ALSO BY MARIE PONSOT

Easy

Springing

The Bird Catcher

The Green Dark

Admit Impediment

True Minds

Collected Poems

Collected Poems

Marie Ponsot

Alfred A. Knopf

New York · 2016

THIS IS A BORZOI BOOK
PUBLISHED BY ALFRED A. KNOPF

www.aaknopf.com/poetry

Knopf, Borzoi Books, and the colophon are registered trademarks of
Random House LLC.

Many of the poems in this collection were previously published in the
following works:

True Minds, copyright © 1956 by Marie Ponsot (City Lights, 1956).
Selected Fables and Tales of La Fontaine, translated by Marie Ponsot
(Signet Classics, 1966). *About Impediment,* copyright © 1981 by Marie
Ponsot (Alfred A. Knopf, 1981). *The Green Dark,* copyright © 1988 by
Marie Ponsot (Alfred A. Knopf, 1988). *The Bird Catcher,* copyright © 1998
by Marie Ponsot (Alfred A. Knopf, 1998). *Springing,* copyright © 2002
by Marie Ponsot (Alfred A. Knopf, 2002). *Easy,* copyright © 2009 by
Marie Ponsot (Alfred A. Knopf, 2009).

Grateful acknowledgment is made to the following publications in which
some of the previously collected poems originally appeared:

*13th Moon, City I, City Lights Review, Columbia, Commonweal, Kenyon
Review, The Little Magazine, The Paris Review, Penny Poems New Haven,
Poetry, America, The New Yorker, Open Places, Phoenix, Shenandoah,
A Shout in the Street, Southwest Review, Western Humanities, Woman Poet:
Northeast, Women's Studies,* and *The Yale Review.*

Library of Congress Cataloging-in-Publication Data
Names: Ponsot, Marie, author.
Title: Collected poems / Marie Ponsot.
Description: First edition. | New York : Alfred A. Knopf, 2016. |
      "This is a Borzoi book."
Identifiers: LCCN 2015046259 | ISBN 9781101947678 (hardcover) |
      ISBN 9781101947685 (eBook)
Subjects: | BISAC: POETRY / American / General.
Classification: LCC PS3531 .O49 2016 | DDC 811/.54—dc23 LC record
available at http://lccn.loc.gov/2015046259

Front-of-jacket photograph courtesy of the author
Jacket design by Chip Kidd

Manufactured in the United States of America

First Edition

Contents

ADMIT IMPEDIMENT (1981)

Admit Impediment

Among Women

Hommages

Discovery

II. *Separate, in the Swim*

III. *The Split Image of Attention*

FROM SPRINGING (2002)

New Poems

Uncollected Poems, 1946–1971

EASY (2009)

I

NEW POEMS (2016)

TRUE MINDS (1956)

TAKE MY DISPROPORTIONATE DESIRE

Enough of expressionist flowers lions and wheat,
Let us consider our separate needs
Here in this beautiful city of delicate surfaces
That a touch makes bleed.

Bring me that truth love-ridden whose black blaze makes
A comfort in the ice-bitten ghettos of cities, that wise
Love whose intemperate told truth thrusts into the aching
Arms of old men old women's lonely bodies with a cry.

All lovers, even lucky, need such intransigence as stays
Wrecked harborers who together cough, drink, spit
Gay blood into the gutter. I need that passion, miracle,
Incautious faith. To only you I offer it.

ANALOGUE

I watch me until I disappear and we
Enter the danced dimension of the good
True beautiful, whose claims may be
Ignored but not withstood.

Join me because forever perfected
Love's one moment emerges here
Forever alive. Time undermines us
But our made love stands clear.

LOVE LETTER

Friend, friend, see how my languor, pleased with romance,
Defeats the burning premise of this all-God day;
For my our sake, be quick, bring on your best bold
Hard intolerance. Say daydreams are fake, and say
We work to make and be. Wake me. With patient rage
Break my mirrors, shake my vanity whose
Bravest best is less by chasms than the beautiful
Calculus this God-made noon exclaims; lose
My placid tepid apathy; loose me; make me advance
My love beyond our love to where love's lovers dance.

"QU'AI-JE À FAIRE EN PARADIS?"

Alexander did not in god's costume recall more
Disquietly Macedonian apples and tame snakes than I,
Fantastically shod with peace and cloaked with love,
Evoke old names for bitterness and hear harsh ghosts cry.

The Persians mocked, though they knelt, his leopard and golden
Skirts and slotted crown that claimed the holy stood
After voyages among their halls. What kneelers laugh
To see me upright here, having cast off sword and hood?

A LA UNE

Let no word with its thinking threat
Thrust betwixt our kissing touch;
The most tenuous shaping breath
Were here too much.

I seek within your single pulse
The golden diametric, whence
Suppress all plural ways to truth,
Suspend all duple evidence.

You do match me. I set
You free. We may yet
Be.

EXTEMPORE

Motion does not halt with stillness,
Sound outlasts a cry;
Brimming toward infinite limits,
They do not die.

Evoked by the echoing cadences
Of your departure and return
My furthest lost distances
Stir to learn

You, my inhabitant, in a more radiant
Retention of light, an intenser air,
More luminous, a last change to mark
Your presence everywhere.

ESPOUSAL

Glad that we love and good at it, we riot in it, brought
To a deafness, wrought up against death, in a live
Striding splendor as we rush through slamming doors.

Hurry, we shout to the tree-soft hills, Part greenly; they
Lapse back; the free rivers trapped at the dam strive
Beautifully to follow the big swathe of our course.

The shot sun leaps; he whirls; he plummets to fall
Cut out of heaven by our bow-hot knives;
He roars down the mountain, breaks on goldrock shores.

Now among the textures of dark we quickly advance
Breathing kisses into shadows as they come alive;
Decorous, delirious, our dancing tramples the felt grass floor.

And the cut-out sun-circle plunges, down it dives;
And fire blazes at the earth's jewel-runneled core.

MATINS AND LAUDS

Excited as a sophisticated boy at his first
Passion of intellect, aware and fully free
Having lost title to full liberty; struck
Aware, for once, as I would always be;

It is day and I still shaken, still sure, see
It is not ring-magic nor the faithing leap of sex
That makes me your woman; marks our free
And separate wills with one intent; sets
My each earlier option at dazzling apex
And at naught; cancels, paid, all debts.
Restless, incautious, I want to talk violence,
Speak wild poems, hush, be still, pray grace
Taken forever; and after, lie long in the dense
Dark of your embrace, asleep between earth and space.

QUEM PERSEQUERIS

This kiss is the question,
This intention for keeps,
This marriage the contest
Where truth, masked, leaps.

Love is of lies
The uncompromised foe.
Until you bless us I
Will not let you go.

CIRCLE, OF FRIENDS

And among us are these, see, the resplendent companions,
Look in the soiled my world how even darkened I reflect
Quick darlings everywhere for love to love; how such
Magnificence among the slums confounds the chart-bound
      architect.

(Not that we are poor but that many lack only love;
therefore a little vine of guilt grows fast,
sapping the cedars where, housed in our marriage, we have
plenty, where our lucky lot is cast.)

And among us are saints. Poor and the poor, the chosen and those
Who choose, one choice may yet hold all wills viced.
One man and his beloved couple in a holy knowing bed and all
Torn joy girls and their takers turn in sleep to Christ.

POSSESSION

You are right. In dreams I might well dance before the Ark.
Coming out of ether I might cry on reed and rood of sacredness.
Yet you should not for that reason suspect altars between us
Nor scent a fear of incense in the cruciform caress.
Marriage is blessed but does not bless.

I warned you before this smoked ground struck your knees,
Saying Be holy, see where the whipped top spins;
Saying This world is that world's mimesis, bloodless
But sensual and we do not even contain our sins.
I said, Betray it and the bedraggled cockerel wins.

Listen. Do you hear? Now he crows.
Now we are going where God knows.

ULTRAMARINE

Clear and strange as an island, the disparate
Light that is the thought of you rose up, was
Lifted up in a travesty of touch and I, desperate,
Whitened, held out wanting hands having
Forgotten the sea between that keeps us separate.

Hope's lust comes in a riptide; the mind is torn
As the air in shock of waves on rocks is flayed
With incessant messages of storm from
Deeper than lamprey or pearl relayed.

Think of the sleep at the center to make tolerable
That deep peace which is the eventual
Encounter of equal forces, immovable,
Massed, still, and equivocal;
But the rock, the island, drifts up free, a
Cold jewel to the sun from under the unlocked sea.

WELCOME

Under the riven battle of a warring night
Lucifer hurtles him hellward, each separate
Star exhorts its galaxy to peace, and you
Come straitly through a thousand storms
Unweaponed to this withheld waiting place.

What other than vigil of crescent and upturning sphere
Have I beyond these arms to offer, what flowered branch
Springs despite storms of ice, what is not scathed or spent?
I am not marked with fervor, am unbound
By circlets of prophecy, unbraceleted; free;
My scarless breasts do not hint at the kniving edge
That need has pressed them to; and my eyes see
Though blind with terror but a splendid hour since.

Yet find me not unwelcoming who has kept
Nothing as garland save these angry arms
Where no one else has slept.

MULTIPARA: GRAVIDA 5

Come to term the started child shocks
Peace upon me; I am great with peace;
Pain teaches primal cause; my bones unlock
To learn my final end. The formal increase
Of passionate patience breaks into a storm of heat
Where calling on you love my heart's hopes rise
With violence to seize as prayer this sweet
Submitting act. I pray. Loud with surprise
Thrown sprung back wide the blithe body lies
Exultant and wise. The born child cries.

PEINE FORTE ET DURE

City not my city that seeing loving I cry
Is holy; people at last made mine: in our dark striking
Love we are twin instruments upholding
Hands and their suspension to the tree.
Naught aches after birth to the world that we
Do not equally suffering fail to forgive, caught
In strict denial of that duplicity which lesser
Lovers deal in, pity.   God speaks.
Thunder bush and stone still speak. Columnar
Fire stalks our waking sleep; downwings the dove
Bids us behold. We in the waiting fall press
Poor and royal flesh to poor and royal flesh, tangent at
Wisdom together, in mortal and terrorless love,
Spun surrounded by chaos, the uttered unknown
That cannot invade.   All else inhabits us.
Lest we fail to distinguish pain from mere pain
We as wheat as grain ripen the word and help
The hoisters hillward to a lifting up. What we need
To know we learn till we become as hammered arch,
Divining rod, as desert cry, as rood, as spear, as reed.

TOWARD A NEW DISPENSATION

Stake him out again, bring chains, haste welders,
Warders; hale him, hot Prometheus, who thought he saw
Man become godly, and the means of power innocent in man.

Spike him eaglewise; hold him, impassioned, impotent,
Beneath downrushing dark hard beaks and claws
Come to communicate the madness of such hope for man.

You, fool, who dared teach freedom and its instruments
(Endlessly potent: words, the trick of fire, the alchemic core
Accomplished, and the pyramos of law) to poor split man,

Call back, command, your folly to go on to triumph terribly;
Set your caught self free. Implement your dream once more;
Work out its final scene; make the dream be: Love man.

HART CRANE
(OR, EVERYMAN, HIS OWN GETHSEMANE)

God with his naked hand made you,
to be set forth separately,
yourself, a spiritual animal,
in actual grace.

A ruthless woman in your hating name
instructed that precise savagery
in cold rite and soft festival
in the leap and the wait.

You claimed faith with the difficult
reason, touched to examine delicately
the lifting of the sensual
in intellectual play.

Darkly brilliant and deliberately strange
you spoke unheard to many, very courteously,
were answered only by the brutal;
you came home no place.

Unseen, your shadow cast a screening of pain
across the backs of all that gallery
who sleeping watched you hunt a tactile
ghost your ghost might make its intimate.

Masque unfeathered, did you not entertain
a concept of harrying yet more splendidly:
your act at daggers in the actual
at last interpenetrate?

NEW ENGLAND SUNDAY

The word as it was written, is spoken, will yet be understood,
For all its clear defenders, bodes no known good
To him whose angry tug would unclapper it abroad, and rape
Our blue wing-folded silence to a less decorous shape.

Let him who has a ringing word come muscled, uncouth, full
Of laughter to the still bell tower; let him be primed to pull
Down a soundburst, and then to jig on yanked feet
Roped to that rhythm, hung high above the tongue-filled street.

COMMUNION OF SAINTS:
THE POOR BASTARD UNDER THE BRIDGE

The arrows of the narrow moon flock down direct
Into that looking heart by Seine walls unprotected.
Moonward the eyes of that hurt head still will
Stare and scarcely see the moonlight spill
Because black Notre-Dame between her towers
Strikes home to him the third of this day's hours
And he, now man, heaped cold afaint
Below the Pont Marie will, with a shout,
Enlist among the triumphant when Poor Saint
Julien's bells will clock out
Four.
       In his rags, unchapleted, almost astray
Among the dead packed all immaculate away
Under the city, he awaits his sentry
The four o'clock moon to warrant for his entry
                        o and pure
The pure in children's ranks by bells immured
In gowns of light will singing telling rise
Unfold their arms impelled without surprise
Will lift up flowered laurel, will walk out
Among their golden singing like a victor's shout
To their triumphant heaven's golden ringing brim
And welcome welcome welcome him.

THE GIVEN GRAVE GROWN GREEN

You chose protection from knowledge, from memory, from the
    stain
Truth leaves where truth has lain with those who weep;
You choose death's bargain; your contracts are closed with the sane.
    Where am I now? I am changing
    The tree in the plain
    Into a flowering tower
    Tall and unquiet to keep
    Your inaccurate wishes
    And your misspent pain.
I learn, I lose, my crowding memory cries
In unwaning surprise: You have not sown, I therefore reap.
I have subtle lovers; I have no allies.
    Where you walk you will wonder,
    Your ringed hand over your eyes,
    If the tower's one live climber
    Will live or fall or leap;
    If a tower can stand that houses
    Your structural lies.
These answers having been foreboded, these things being known,
The blown branch will grow quiet, the root like rock strike deep,
The plain will offer the tower, open and alone.
    Where you are you can follow
    The leaves turning to stone,
    The living branch made patient,
    The trunk attaining sleep;
    You can watch from your closed window
    How true false love has grown.

FORMAL

Reassert the learner's strictness;
Spine the crooking back;
Welcome careful application
Of the readjusting rack.

Search out the skeleton,
Structurally sound;
Least willed, most common,
A given ground.

Test out its alignment, prove
Joint and bone and groove;
If need be,
Rack the memory.

AMPHISBAENIC

Christ be corrupt in me if I cause to fall
The wall beyond whose height I hear you weep
Outside. Somewhere.

Your name betrays me back to blackness; appalled,
I lie lost in a pride of lions, asleep,
Smiling, unaware.

Christ be corrupt in me if I will or build a wall
Beyond whose height I might not hear you weep
Any you. Any where.

Guilt for betrayal dates back to a little stall,
A newborn child, a woman half asleep,
Intolerably aware.

Christ my last place of safekeeping is all
Riddled with holes and still I keep
Everything there.

DOWNTOWN

Surprised, the pursy woman sees, pauses to sham
Disdain for my folly who am laughing still
Because the sun's fierce glory roared, to damn
All murk forever, an instant before it fell.

The street is a passageway dedicated to the alive,
The being beauty of man and child; I take
Toll of their lived-in walking; I thrive
On the grace and gaucherie they, moving, make.

Always among them there is one whose glancing face, unasked,
Fantastic, says, here is a friend of angels; masked,
Yet unmistakable the bright middle creatures move ablaze
About us; and make the intelligence leap with praise,
Rush to claim a breaking joy from joy's created trace

o good world, God's work, turn, turn, turn in place
Wide in the wild eternal air of His embrace.

SUBJECT

We but begin to hope to know, having known
The no-man's echo of your knowing voice;
We barely claim we have chosen,
Naming our choice.

To feast your coming it is you who must prepare;
Given your love we dare not not care;
Wherefore spare not spare us not
Do not spare.

"WHAT ARE YOU DOING HERE, STEPHEN?"

Lean walkers on light feet connive
At splendor, fail, get by another chance
Truth's best children, though bastard, born alive,
Born rehearsing the modes of need, the sleeping dance.
Before the pivotal altar, between bright horn and holy horn,
Step the cherished, cheating innocents, sweetly stepping, capricorn.

They improvise to flute them, who have gone too far:
The instructed musicians, responsible, are their servants secular.

Moving always, and wary, making an arc
Across straight streets, shy at shadow or post,
Half halting, half smiling, breathless, they hark.
These kneeling think ellipses, square the circled host,
Rise heavy and gaudy with wine, a new pain held in the head;
They go out graceful and laborless, greeding, easy, capriped.

They feed them, pouring, whose own thirst shuts their throats:
Impatient waiters, forfeit in their many-colored paid-for coats.

CONTINGENT

Whose less amatory intellects discern
That in each petaled particular
Whole fields of flowers burn;
Whose ideas of fields are
Radiant images on space
Opening to immure
The circle sided and
The lune its quadrature,

These are your champions; they
Will deduce what I, less wise,
Can but enjoy; their prized
Incisive reasons will rephrase
Your darkless mercy and
Your grace its blaze;
Their metaphysic may communicate
Why I silent kneel amazed.

Yet let them use my useless
Joyous speechless cry
As a nothingworth of clue,
A trace, though faint and wry,
Of your perfections:
You know that I
But live in you, yet you
Let me not die.

TO THE AGE'S INSANITIES

Shriek said the saw smile said the mice
Come said the tall crowfooted bright
Bareheaded boy I won't call twice.

Twist said the tongue leap said the toe
Leave said the seaman arched in fright
One of this crew has got to go.

Spit said the thorn kiss said the tree
But Peace cried I loud in the night
You are my freedom. And they let me be.

ST. PAUL AND THE HEART'S HARRIERS

Lack not anger; hide not that rare pure
Rush of rage to the heart but ranting
Grant that love needs pity's fury,
See where, loosed, love's dark hawk rises, hunting.

Who has not hunted will not recognize
The hunt's sure poise, the perilous tilt;
May be held scrupulous by mockbird's cries;
They lie who love not. Be angry. Lack guilt.

EASTER SATURDAY, NY, NY

Confusion of bells, and all the starling sky
Is shouting, even the gloved policemen are laughing
Because you turn again.

You chose despair, were darkened, now changed you
Chosen veer; you choose; you are; God knows
There's no despair could quiet you. There is
This afterward, this new now abolishing
Your proven death   o darling
How the city rings with light, sheer
Stone is diamond, all perfect squares
Flare into tropics of flowers, the rush of the roller
Skating children tunnels into singing. Our
Loss, impeached, dies off clever and devious;
It was too magic, too untrue. Triumph
Up the avenue sounds trumpets and roses;
The tallest buildings blaze all night and dancing
Is everywhere under the sidestreet trees.

ROCKEFELLER THE CENTER

Roland is dead and the ivory broken
Marie has forgotten the limb-striking end of joy.

    Pigeons patter, whirr, at the copy cathedral; a Prometheus
    Aeschylus did not intend submits to sparrows, less than
           ever free;
    At his manufactured feet the delicate ice skaters swirl.

    A paralleled curve incised among angles, the splendid loose
    Avenue ripples with peopled cars, and the figuring girl
    Looks at the sky beyond the sidewalk's ginko tree.

Though the sea-coves echo with innumerable
Voices no man suspects the vanished Nereids.

Artemis at midnight is
No longer solicited.

ADMIT IMPEDIMENT (1981)

For

Mary Denver Candee

Marie Candee Birmingham

Monique Ponsot Rudnytsky

Tara Rudnytsky

Deborah Ponsot

Danielle Ponsot

Let me not to the marriage of true minds
Admit impediments . . .

—William Shakespeare

Admit Impediment

FOR A DIVORCE

I
Death is the price of life.
Lives change places.
          Asked why
we ever married, I smile
and mention the arbitrary fierce
glance of the working artist
that blazed sometimes in your face

but can't picture it;

I do recall (1) shoes you left
in my closet, echoing worn-out
Gauguin; (2) how once under down
drugs I roared at you Liar! oh liar!
exulting in not lying
                    ((as if
I'd made a telltale drawing . . .)

2
How dear how undark appear the simple
apparently simple wishes of the untried will;
how dark it is here and how
suddenly too still.

3
Glad I need not chance again
against your prone packed weight
my uncertain stance,
I giddy with relief
relax into mobility.

.   .   .

The state we made of love,
that you fled out of
empty-handed,
I have enlarged
into a new mainland geography
where I move as if unburdened where
my burdens bear me.
You said once I had
taught you human speech.
I am glad
I never taught you to dance.

4
Or, perhaps I drove you to flight.
Perhaps (freckled) islanded
I (skinny) was Circe;
Aiaia sounds familiar and
even on my crystal sands even
under my fragrant trees you
were a pig

a pig, and I a Circe stupefied who
could not tell the master from the man,
tusk-torn because too slow to know
I had in choosing you

dismissed Odysseus
and the luck of Odysseus and
his mind immune to magic

for a prentice hand the sea could tame,
a poor sailor, lotus changeling, destined
never to come home.

. . . or so let me flatter myself,
fabulously.

5
But if the fable go that way, it goes on,
to say that in myths gross beasts must
wound; it is their work; by this work
mere moon-starred magicians may turn in
to useful plainer day's-eye citizens
                    and so, that blind
                    boar whose tusks wound
                    becomes a cruel kind
of guide or christ, an unwilling
saviour, greedy to the hurt that,
necessary, healed to a shiny scar,
serves to teach
identify or save.
And should this be the case
I wish I could say I'd rendered you such grace.

6
                    (. . . a drawing telltale
& pure as one of yours when you drew edged
objects—a bird, a wheel—in the shift
of the light they turn in; as you drew
the soft unpierced air that bore
sounds of wings and waters at Banyuls
where we sunstruck went up under the arch
where we came upon fountains))
                    and now
exactly I do
darkly I do
        recall the you of then when
every time you touched me it was true.

7
Deaths except for amoeba articulate
life into lives, separate, unnamed, new.

Not all sworn faith dies. Ours did.
(1) I am now what I now do.
(2) Then in me
that stunning lover
          was you.

NEW YORK: APPENDIX OF PREDECESSORS

I

People, I offer all my options, see,
Sweepstakes tickets, wishbones, beans, boxtop offers,
Ranked by threes in rows of three

A lifetime collection,
Everything I've got,
Take the whole lot

And grant one wish
Preceded by a general please: Please,

Everyone stop dying
Just for a while a week do not
Rattle, throat sick of speech; bang
Steady, pulse thready and thinning;
Bullets, sleep in the chamber;
Accidents, be righted; infants, insist,
Accept the running blaze of breath
For now. Patience, Death.

Grant relicts this, give us ellipsis,
Time to count heads, catch up,
Or! if a week's too long wait just
An instant, stay, all stay;

Let the lately dead complete their exits;
Let me for once mourn well the
Stop of unstopped body as the person disassociates
And we are left to burn or bury what we can.

2

Born abed,
Bedded wedded,
Dead in bed;
We at any wakes and weddings weep it with
The one kind of tears; absurd they replace
All we have lost of the old charms; our one
Remaining Woman's Tabu: the Wedding Warning:
We use such tears to convey;
So to weep stuns.

Wakes are the worst weeping though.

O my blood.
Does nothing ever die.
Body more than body
Does no body ever die.

I watch over this disembodied body.
I learn how the new dead lie.
Wakes are ceremony, crazed.
Grief is an elemental air
The ungrieved cannot breathe.
So dumb is sympathy. The shocked
Stand to stupefy all comers who stare
No wonder like runners
Of long long hills
Whose, Sorry for your trouble,
Is a gasp like swallowed laughter
And the answer's desperate.

3

My father a man gave
A great shout and
Rearing up died.

.   .   .

Unfair, Pelican, o most
Unpitying to hurry so
To be unoccupied.

No fault of his. Mind,
I'm not ungrateful. Now
I'm landed gentry just like him.
He left me
Everything:
A strong box; a jest book
A sketch book and especially
Unfashionably a fat book
Of tender memories, all three
Mint, in boards, unfoxed, indeed
Unread, he is so dead.
In the box, securities,
Gilt-edged; some golden deeds;
And one note of hand owning
His wealth to be ambiguous,
An appendix to the fat book
Of predecessors he died debtor to,
Whose elegies yet to be written
He intended to have set
In granite when he got the time.

    What, friend! fresh out of time?
    Here, here's some of mine.
    Your heir, I can give
    What you cannot refuse or take,
    A privilege of those who live.
Let me reckon up
What I may recuperate.

4
Cut a first stone.
Cut, for my father's Edwardian father,

Whose son 8 years old at 8 a.m.
Found him gorgeously asprawl
Inverse like Peter, resplendent in
Aureoles of haemorrhage, arms & coat
Flung open backward down the brownstone stairs:
>   Jack Birmingham, young John that was,
>   Invented for redemption
>   The coupon label; his estate
>   Includes 2 gross of mandolins,
>   3 of ukeleles, and some mixed
>   American premium guitars;
>   Jack, who gambled for sons
>   On a bride small-boned but arrogant,
>   Whose gamble paid off in thirteen children
>   Of whom three survived, one a son.
Nothing now no one will do justice
To enterprise, hard wit, fast choice,
A life lived laughing urging his pockets
To pleasure in big engraved cash dollars,
Though in his son my father's book I read
What years his hopes despaired on waking,
Knowing his father would not say again
The sentences he must have bubbled hot to no ear
Hung head down, into his fur coat collar,
Trying to make time teach us
How to say our morning prayers.

5
Old Calvary the Cemetery holds,
Among his parents grand and great
And the many small white boxes, his bones.
Aunt Dannie saw to it (Anne, not Danielle,
Daughter of Michael a hero
Of the fiery City, Brooklyn,
An honorary everything Volunteer), Anne
The shirt-waisted maiden, tortoise-
Shell combs in folded redgold hair, First

Woman Buyer for Stern's Department Store,
And never missed a day not even the day
They buried him her brother very decently
According to arrangements she had made.
It says here she deserved
A hill-capping Parthenon
But had no taste for thanks.

6

Kate comforted.
Kate (Katie to no one but the dead,
A sister, a second at most mourner)
Shawled the pain-stiff widow in a chair;
Tied the girls' ribbons and made the boys dress warm,
Admired snowmen often after school
Until evening, that bitter year,
Then called the children in, shook
Ashes down to bring the flames up,
Poured rounds of cocoa hot,
Counted them by name like kingdoms
Saying, "Mary how lucky you are, all
Within and none without, my dear!"

7

Summers came, one to memorialize Great
Uncle Jake (who south for the gone war
Fell, woke in a true clement meadow,
Became a Kentucky cooper taking unto him
A Kentucky beauty tall and lame); he
Many decades at peace came
Home to them with August
Walked across the bridge to Brooklyn
And invested in presents of ice cream sodas
Himself carrying vanilla and chocolate metal
Pails of them & trailing a ten-year-old boy
Who never forgot that hot afternoon
Up Berry Street striding, both hands tense

On the thin handle of a brimming strawberry third.
Jake took what a man with a niece can,
Pride, in gay-as-silks Mary perched
Neat, bright, unwinged on her rocker,
Her body brittle with arthritis and loss,
More broken than his mare-tossed wife's,
Her wide mouth between bites of pain
Calling her children to her
With jokes, promises of paradise,
Nonsense, and words to the wise.

Needing their love
A woman not fond
Not gifted with a mother tongue,
She learned to entertain,
Determined to see the girls grown
And her one son place his stakes forever
Outside that house of women
On a woman of his own.
(Mother, that was you, that girl
Then twelve to be for twelve years courted.)
Upon hearing that I
His child was born, Mary
Clapped her hands and flew
Entirely out of time.

8
Blurred generations of women,
Our expent medians, you leave us
In confusion in your debt.
We ignore of you woman
For woman why you were not witless
Half your hearts with all your dead
And half vicarious, attendant
On the triumphs of the live.
Groggy with joy and grief,
Infirm, analphabet, allowed for,

How was it you held steady
Without franchise where you stood
At the last extremity of love?
That house of women thrived on watching
Wishing pretty Rettie well, as she alone
Became a real turn-of-the-century girl,
Typist, teacher, lively, perhaps
Too intense. Home she came
Through downtown traffic, humming,
In a carriage hired by her last school
After something slick as birds
Splitting the air flew beaked
Through her and her racing heart.
Twenty, "I'm going to die, why not
Like this," she sang waltzing
Alone to the tune like her "The Beautiful
Blue Danube" too sweet too brief unripe
Rushing to a dizzied close.
One New York noon she put on gloves
Hat and veil, humming, and strode
Uphill to St. Someone's Gothic pile
And died,
That way, why not.

9
They tried
To remember her, what a soft lot
They were, copying out of love
Her light-catching wit, and what
They caught of it was her dire joy
Transparent to certain pain.
Kate the comforter at dusk for her
Went sometimes to the unblinded window
Saying softly, "Hark!"   Even
Thirty years later, delirious, her hips
Broken falling into what children
Fear, the cellar dark, Kate

Laughed like a girl, in a girl's
Unshaken voice cried plainly, "Rettie!
Oh! what fun." So Kate died,
Comforted.

10

Dead man, I cannot read your note of hand.
I cannot remember every anything you said.
So this anecdotal tree must stand
Gut-rooted, stemmed in the breast,
And branched in the brain and hand
To arbor honest grief
Until grief dies to understand
(As superstitions—like rock to sand—
Rot into the bottom soil of true belief)
How I am your triumph as phoenix
Whom I weep as pelican.

BASIC SKILLS

Crazy chopped shrieks of school
people penned in the scarred
yard stop at the metal
whistle blown hard.

Exposed among monitors, at
angles marked in the concrete,
the children shrink. Teaching
screaming & cringing, the raw
teacher screams above
a selected 8-year-old boy.

What's outside the shiny
web fence is invisible,
unofficial, its random strengths
—natural hugs, curious energy,
all that only age of gold—
for these lead-alchemic hours gone
into the jailsteel boundary
taken in & glinting
like tears behind eyes he shuts, as
the head of the boy goes down.

DE RELIGIONE HUMANITATIS VERA

       Hear us,
God of man's desire and will;
Maker and magnet, be near us
Who again plan to kill.

Lord of Man Destroyer of Man
Lord Slaughter we confess you
Our lives exalt your cause.

We adore you, o best, and we bless you.
Behold: with our precious gifts
We reinforce your word.
Deign to receive them:
   energy; passion; treasure;
   these persons to priest you:
   our dearest well-grown boys.
Sworn dying or killing to pleasure you
They vow to propagate your joys.

Rapt, enrapt with power, a far-darting
Light-swift, phantom-borne host, they
Lift up skill-hallowed hands:
      Maker of peace,
High priest and first principle,
Instruct them that their hands may
Worthily bestow you on those
We have chosen for you today.

We are yours, Lord War; you know it.
Shaped to your image our hearts
Are open to you, and open
The works of our days.
No matter what we have written,

What other gods we may praise,
We celebrate no mystery
But yours; it is your law we obey.
Our dreams, our doings, and our history
Witness you. Wherefore we pray:

Let the killer priests of our killer race
Go forth like justice blind to the kill
According to your will.

Let the rite of ruin prove
What our hearts ripe
For ruin believe.
O Father of Nations,
Gladly we perceive
Your glory performed:
Our acts of worship re-create
The substance of the archetype
In our own idiom. We elevate
     the failure of the woman
     who with her single body
     is trying to safesurround
     her several children; nearby
     intact with agony an old
     man sits on the ground
        our gentle sons
     have blasted in your name;
     they return to blast it again.

The skin of the children like peach
Skin splits and the fine flesh is
Giving us joy in you as we
Give them you, Lord Death.

This fresh decade of children
Takes shock of us; our skilled sons
See to it; they shock infants,

Innocence, local ignorance,
Into the perpetual
Newness of your ritual.

What they do is the best we can.
Their worship is ours, God of the Race of Man.

We offer the blood of their and our priests,
The blood of those the priests represent,
Lifeblood, theirs and ours. Better,
We who desire the spilling thereof
Offer our desire, our world's will bent
On becoming as your instrument
In the spilling of blood
As with garments of radiance, undulant,
With garments of sheer fire,
Our sons clothe the live children.

We exult as our sons become
According to the ardor of these acts
Your men forever, having sunk in you
The roots of their manhood, Lord Slaughter,
Their love for you absolute,
Once done all done,
Your servants henceforth, Lord War,
In whom
        all men are one.

THE ALIEN EXAMINERS

"Here is a rational
beast agile at the thumb
ignorant, concupiscent,
and steeped in lethargy.

"Here is a he of the kind
which casts up institutions
that they pollute & cast down;
more plentiful than pebbles,
more complex, these fabrications
are all based on two or three
nightmares of the family.

"Note the sight apparatus: predictable
organically apparently nothing new.
But if we examine the retina
we find non-repeating patterns,
unique ones, like fingerscrolls;
we find no two alike! Therefore no two
samples see the same, as when they touch
no two samples sense the same.
Infinite difference! Wonderful.

"Ask him what he sees.
He is not necessarily dumb.
Most have a kind of language
they jump in & out of, to hide
as well as to keep facial muscles
supple for food intake. Sounds
they hear often they may repeat. Ask."

"What do you see?"
        "You've got me ass-up, mates.
        I'd answer better on my own two feet."

RESIDUAL PARALYSIS

for June Jordan

I'm an unable woman who loves to dance
but my polio leg won't go, or will
a while, until yanked by muscle cramps
that grip the ankle so it gives way
& locks twisted, perpendicular. And then
of course the damned thing's sprained, fat, blue, & wrong.

When I hear music I think nothing's wrong
that I can't manage, and I start to dance,
inside at first, smiling for the beat; then
the sound strides up my back & claims it will,
if I let it, float me safe all the way
on the long waves of high style nothing cramps.

So I'm a chump, surprised, betrayed by cramps,
ashamed to admit I have something wrong
until it's too late & rhythm drains away.
Let drop, I fall untuned outside the dance
insulted in the body of the will
to hold control, that cooled my fever then.

That I was sick, I kept half secret then.
Years of vanity, vain practice, vain cramps
got me walking even downstairs at will.
I valued that, my false claim, "Nothing's wrong!
(I can't press down a clutch and I can't dance
but) I'm not lame (not very, anyway)."

Lies have small voice where dancing has its way;
old true tales sweeten into the now of then
which is the breathing beat of every dance;
the wrecks & twists of history uncramp
into trust that present kindness can't go wrong
among warm partners of a common will.

.　.　.

I try. If I can stop lying, I will.
I'll claim my cramps & limit them that way,
trust and forget my history, right & wrong,
while others dance. I might, less vain than then,
forgive dead muscles & relax their cramps.
I can love dancing from outside the dance.

When trust uncramps the ordinary will
to laugh its way past accidental wrong,
those outside then step inside the dance.

SONG, FROM THEOPHRASTUS

Struggle makes its own strict sense.
The will kept sharp keeps free,
Learns reflex skill, cuts out pretense
    (the eye in the reed, the joint in the vine,
    the knot in the tree)
Dark evidence beneath the bark
Stars the wood where the heavily
Fruited branches rose and left a mark
    (the eye in the reed, the joint in the vine,
    the knot in the tree)
The thick-rimmed notch sustains
Grapes lustering toward wine
To bear the beat and weight of rains
    (the knot in the tree, the eye in the reed,
    the joint in the vine)
Rushes raise up a thread-spined length
In the union of their thrust toward seed,
Rooted and grounded in flimsy strength
    (the joint in the vine, the knot in the tree,
    the eye in the reed)
Bones unbroken lack the core,
The doubled strength of bones that be
Knitted to themselves once more
    (the eye in the reed, the joint in the vine,
    the knot in the tree)

ABOUT MY BIRTHDAY

I'd like to assume,
from my April birthday,
I quickened the womb
on the 4th of July.

If you suffered as I
a sternly fought tendency
to endless dependency
you'd know why.

SCRIPT FOR A HOME MOVIE
of the first Joyce Symposium, Dublin

I reeling with labyrinthitis from the tricks
of a new zoom super-8 was trying to disc
—over over & over (peep. tip.) Dublin
at the dearest Joyce Symposium composed
of June Jimlovers, scholar gossips,
boilers of his holy bones . . .

& here they are, at UCD, a lecture hall,
a lecturer, singing "The Lass of Antrim."
Here's some rubble, smallfar; zap
under wallpaper flowers paling flapping;
and a dropback presenting
elegant Eccles Street still foursquare.

Here I'd a midwife companion (Oxon.). See her
bagbearing half a mile off on Sandymount Strand
AND GULLS TAKE TO
SIDESLICING FLIGHT FOR HER TOSSING THEIR
NAMINGS OF AIR down & up with Howth distant; pan,
to the right's the rim of, & here close it's the

Martello Tower! a circle of sun, stone-ringed;
the generous head bent to listen is FRANK
Budgen & the gentle lady of him KIND IN
CONVERSE with American academics; look beyond
now upSURGING Giorgio bursts german-
speaking out of the Stephenhole joining
them JOYCEAN WITH (o the image of his father,
accdg to Mz Veyl) his cheerful snarl graven

as against the plashsoft sky heads turn to watch
(pan) where among rocks among seachurn 3 boys

run to dive, dive,

        dive

           in.

Here the spacespoil
zoomer dizzied me, here
hackles rose on those atop
the tower   among whom then

                was heard
                the last

laugh from the live haunt of him
whose known to be transalpine bones
do not keep him from these stones
he shaped to build our Babel from.
Now too my
hackles rise
reviewing his projected shadow thrown
MENE on my wall to show
faint stains of intellectual abuse.
Well
PENANCE for imprudence
for having had the effrontery to
use a long booklove as excuse:
I go to black to do.

BILINGUAL

Languages before they are words
or systems are persons speaking
and persons spoken to. The bilingual
cannot, for example, convey in English,
"Au placard, la lavande
fait bien blanchir les linges";
there's no American woman to whom
it could be said.

The pain of having two languages comes from a
straining between them in the mind,
from a need to keep them separate and
a desire, forbidden, dangerous,
to marry them: like twins who
safely unentwined by each other's presence
stress their differences
and who when absent cannot but represent
longing for union of the purest kind.

The two tongues must be untrue to each other.
Their speaker always has one mute mouth kept pressed
closed against the barrier and already possessed
of other words to word each word better,
that the speaking one is deaf to.

Dreams give relief but no rest.
Both babble there, each other's audience,
making love eloquent at last, coupling
with the rich attention grand passion
gives in slowness to the body of the lover;
there the American answers, with pleasure,
"I love the smell of lavender."

FAITHFUL

always on the job, dependable   your wild self/your wisewoman/your friend
I am, like you, a burden bearer;   I too keep a skinned grip on this minute as
I comfort, you comfort me.   watch out!
steady on, brother ass!   a sweet slick beast, solo,
look   our encounter   darts out from between our hands
(so plain we don't believe in it)   flashes upward strongly
sustains us as we plod heavily   toward the ground of our great longing
far apart, not where we'd thought to be   where it runs free
not knowing my labor strengthens you   timelessly
not knowing your labor strengthens me   if we love the grip
we see our comfort does not stale or tempt   or time or trap
us to quit, grab the chance, & flee.   we feel free
maybe they meet deepest who must work to see   if we love the trap enough
maybe we do believe, if secretly   we leap free.
                Dear my companion
      never to be   let the sweet beast
          keep free

"SOIS SAGE Ô MA DOULEUR"

I
Here they are, what you hid,
what shamed you, the
secrets of your life in cardboard
cartons at my feet (your
life you laid no claim to)
gifts, accomplishments, genius,
and what you did with these.

Here is the cast-off evidence,
amassed, earned, dry—
I read aghast through thousands
of pages of claims
you earned and hid and
did not choose to make
or did not make
or, no one heard you make

            while you made
dinner, jokes, love, kids'
tuition money, friends, the most
of dim situations,
and the best of everything.

You are extreme, being you & dead,
your beginning & end extremely visible;
but the dereliction of your crowded cartons
many women know
(and some men
who live like younger
sons or girls or saints—
but most who expect nothing
for work well done

are women) especially
women of my generation
—almost famous almost exemplary
almost doctors almost presidents almost
powerful, women entirely
remarkable, entirely unremarked,
            women with dues paid
            who lay no claim to what they've paid for
            and are ashamed
            to be ashamed to lay a claim.

I cry telling a woman (like you but
like me still alive, taking that chance)
of your secret works and unbanked treasury.
Redfaced I blow my nose & we
exchange stares her face stripped by insight
back from forty to fourteen; she knows;
the rose-petal peony of her snaps in a
jump-cut back to a bud, she looks
bud-tight, slices of white petal showing,
slowest to open where there is no sun;
there is no sun; our secret is your secret;
we see what we have done.
We see your life. It hurts us.
It is our life. There are many like us.
We have daughters; they have daughters.
What are we to do?   Many
and many like us would mock us if they knew
that we who mistrust power & will not compete for it
conceive of other claims but only in pain conceive
that we might make them.

. . . died at fifty. Is fifty young?
It is young. You died too young.
Dead woman, this side of despair
where I use you to say I care,
does knowing what we can't help

help? or was the absence of answer
fatal, was that the infarction
that sprung your heart apart?
did the infected heart, healed, fall loose again helpless,
did our helplessness prevent your breath
as you lay in wait for the too-late ambulance
until you drew an answer for us with your death?

What model did we who are like you give you?
none. One of us, as good as you a scholar,
worships to complete her late husband's opera; one
slips hand to mouth modestly and paints
essential paintings, goes on painting, who
sees it? only a few; as for me I start out
but everything I encourage to happen
keeps me from finishing

I do not write your name here
because it would hurt me;
you would have hated it; you deserve
silence for failure who had
silence for your excellence.
You had got used to that, made each success
a smaller plant in a smaller garden with less light,
and concealed among its leaves the stalks of suffering
perfectly unbudded, the sleekest secret.

Oh, no one discouraged you; many loved you,
everyone liked you, why not, so generous, oh the
parties; some did blame you obscurely: why
were you—gifted, rich—not famous?
That echoed in you,
didn't it; hurt your heart;
made your breath shorten with anxious guilt.

Step by step your breathless death accuses us.
The cartons found in your attic

full of your successful procedures
accuse us whose products are like yours
kept left-handed, womanly secondary
according to the rules. Whose rules?
How can we keep our hot
hatred of power
from chilling into impotence? You
could have disbarred the rules if anyone
had noticed you in time behind them.
With your costly help can we undo
the rules and with or without shame
lay our claims?
Should we who can be happy picturing
who we are, burst alive out of that frame
in our daughters' names?
I say
I am too old, tired, crazy, cold—to
say nothing of ashamed—
to try.
At my feet
your insistent cartons, their danger
implicit, speak or sing in
tongues or invisible flames.

2

Q: Brought to book at last,
    what did you say on your day
    after death, how did you
    sum up your argument?

A: This far side of dying there is no time
    for distance, and so no irony.
    I had to be plain; I said:
I was not a success.
I buried my treasures and lost the maps,
stewardess of my obscurity.
My life was comfortable, easy;

I was lucky; my one triumph was
to experience the world as holy
and to find that humorous.

I was beautiful by strict standards
for each age; dressed well, moved well.
I did not use my beauty.
I liked to be sexual; was shy until
I gave a good partner the pleasure
of teaching me. I made no capital of sex.

I was a wife, supportive, cordial, a helpmeet
and ornament; bore healthy children, mothered
them, improvised; entertained in-laws
as god-sent; kept up our correspondence;
was a presentable hostess, a lab-sharp cook,
a welcomer. Gratefully oh gratefully
I found I was married to a friend.

I came to terms with my family inheritance,
all of it; it did not merit me anything.
I loved my brother. I saw my friends.

I was a good student; women professors
dying left me their libraries & lonely valuables;
played Chopin when asked & Rameau when alone;
had ideas; did not turn intelligence into power.

I liked parties; liked drinks with one friend,
listening; celebrated epiphany; when I was ill
the interns took coffee breaks at my bedside
& told me their specialties;
I submitted to remedy.

Indoors my amaryllis rose yearly in crowds of flowers.
Blue gentians grew outside my country house,
and arbutus fragrant in early spring.
In my last years I watched the coming

and going, predictable & predictably
full of surprises, of birds
on the east-coast flyway. I understood
that they came & went of necessity yet
unaccountably, in mixed flocks, in their
various plumage, unaccountable.

I wrote stories, poems, journals, a serious novel;
no one surely not I saw them to praise them
enough to make them public;
I wasted my Guggenheim. My dissertation
on a fierce Frenchwoman was accepted with praises;
I did not type a clean copy, did not submit it,
was not awarded a final degree; I kept
all these papers secret, a private
joke I had no laughter for.
I wrote no reproaches.

I understood my jobs; employers cherished
their fractions of me, praised & used me.
My work was serviceable, subordinate.

I played the parts given me as
written, word-perfect; I never
laid claim to a part, do not know
what would have happened
had I laid a claim.

I was a quick study; I was not a star.

My only excuse lies in what I
observed of the birds; it is faulty;
it shouldn't apply.

Since I was not a success
I must have been a failure.
There is no one to blame
but myself.

Among Women

AMONG WOMEN

What women wander?
Not many. All. A few.
Most would, now & then,
& no wonder.
Some, and I'm one,
Wander sitting still.
My small grandmother
Bought from every peddler
Less for the ribbons and lace
Than for their scent
Of sleep where you will,
Walk out when you want, choose
Your bread and your company.

She warned me, "Have nothing to lose."

She looked fragile but had
High blood, runner's ankles,
Could endure, endure.
She loved her rooted garden, her
Grand children, her once
Wild once young man.
Women wander
As best they can.

SUMMER SESTINA

for Rosemary

Her daylilies are afloat on evening
As their petals, lemon- or melon-colored,
Dim and lift in the loosening grip of light
Until their leaves lie like their shadows, there
Where she had hid dry corms of them, in earth
She freed of stones, weeded, and has kept rich.

With dusk, the dense air rises unmixed, rich,
Around our bodies dim with evening;
Creek air pours up the cliff to her tilled earth
And we swim in cool, our thoughts so colored
They can haunt each other, speechless, there
Where bubbles of birdsong burst like mental light,

Among the isles of lilies soaked with light.
We wait for moonrise that may make us rich
With the outsight of insight, spilling there
On her meadow when the moon ends evening
And brings back known shapes, strangely uncolored,
To this earthly garden, this gardened earth.

Deep deep go these dug fertile beds of earth
Where mystery prepares the thrust for light.
Years of leaf-fall, raked wet and discolored
With winter kitchen scraps, make the mix rich;
The odds against such loam are evening,
Worked on by her intentions buried there.

Why she does it is neither here nor there—
Why would anyone choose to nurture earth,
Kneel to its dayneeds, dream it at evening,
Plan and plant according to soil and light,
Apple, basil, snowpea, each season rich—
What counts isn't that her world is colored

. . .

Or that by it our vision is colored,
But that the gardener who gardens there
Has been so gardened by her garden: grown rich,
Grown fruitful, grown to stand upon the earth
In answer to the ordering of light
She lends to us this August evening.

By her teaching there we are changed, colored,
Made ready for evening, reconciled to earth,
Gardened to richness by her spendthrift light.

CURANDERA

In New York cold, few command the waking of spring.
When it is winter it is always winter
For those born New Yorkers who crouch mute over
The stains of hurt they hide to advertise.

But Spanish people in overcoats come,
Personal with their heavy dismay,
To the daughterless lady;
They are clouds that cannot rain here;
She hands them broken white
Candles to put lit like crocus at her windows;
Among them her spirit spins mercurial;
The winds freshen; the sky stoops.
        She thinks about helping, thinks
        Where to shop for the white rose,
        The white bird, in the proper places
        Sets saucers of water on the floor
        Of her Queens house where stereo
        Plays the drums. No dirt floor. No hibiscus.

Often her clothing is white. At times she wears
Spangles as only a woman of virtue can. Her round neck
Is ringed with the white beads of the Merciful
And the red and blue beads of Helper Barbara;
Gold links ring her waist to honor Poverty Champion
Who protects the Seven Great Potentials and us from them.
There are eleven Helpers; she can undertake
Eleven dances to introduce Help to those
Who are clean in the way a tree is clean
During the night of a dancing, inside the Florida
Water ring sprinkled on the floor.
A dancing is a trance she takes.
Sweating cleanses.

If visited so as to become her holy Familiar
She stamps as she turns & smokes his favorite cigar;
Rhythms flow from her high welcoming hand down off as He
Laughs in her throat to clear it for his voice:

"The mourning dove has black feet because the pink & green
    blessing of daybreak on it must be supported.
In the box of candles keep always more than seven on a shelf
    higher than shoulder level. Abundance. Respect.
Never cut across the feathers of the throat.
If there is in this house broken glass it must be removed.
If there is in this house a mirror even in a bag it must be
    covered with a white cloth.
Do not beat on the gates; knock, and be ready."

The dismayed comes out of his overcoat jigging & the moving
Opening of doing keeps going changing
Climate into younger weather in
To the break of day. Relief.

FROM THE FOUNTAIN AT VAUCLUSE

1

This light is water. In emerald ascent
Pooled at the cliff it has chiseled, it has brought
To light its clear, unsounded affluent.
To its star-planet I am astronaut
Come home. Crowds come with me, intent
On holiday at the Fountain of Vaucluse.
Its vulnerable air brings us up short.

A girl dips her foot in, holding her shoes.
A boy throws stones so splashes distort
The pool; most males do, as if they confuse
Marking with marring; as if, innocent,
Inept at awe, they smash what they can't use
Or ignore, here where joy's intelligent
In the still light bodied by greening blues.

2

My heart steadies here, sensing something taught:
I take this pool holding opening as
The font and vulva of the planet, brought
From depth to light by the soft force it has
And from view to vision by the path it wrought,
Unknown, central, central, earth-old, blue, blue.
They nod to see it, women on the grass:
Some cross the crown of sunlit stone it wells up through
To watch how limpidly it lets light pass
Transparent to itself. Girls stare who,
Women-trained not to catch but to be caught,
Are not able to shout, throw, sprawl askew.
Here, their malfunction works in them like thought
Transcending the loss of all they do not do.

3

Or so it seems, as girls without parade
Bend to the shoreline, cup their hands, and drink.
Two old women hand themselves down and wade.
Some girls with brothers throw stones; most shrink
As the waters break. They may be afraid
Of breaking anything: *and that is right*
Though praise for it negates what are, we think,
The claims of power. As woman, I take fright
At power in brute strength (here at the blue brink
Of star-borne paradise) which breeds the fight
I shirk but know my people can't evade
While the good, self-bound in either covert spite
Or child-like impotence, watch their good fade.
Landscape be my lens. Rectify my sight.

4

Cockerel, brash, these July boys & men
Cannot love what they have never seen
Or see what pecking greed keeps hid from them,
Trained not to listen for what their lives mean
But to beat. By that blinding stratagem
All lose. Women and men confuse success
With loud failure to work and work serene.
Boys we raise to thrive under cockpit stress,
Faced here with peaceful force, must intervene.
A child trammeled in heeled shoes and ironed dress
Smiles for the blue pool, climbs close to it; then
Her hand if timid touches its face. Yes
I hate her heels and pleats. But praise is sudden
In me for her easy move of tenderness.

5

Another male; three stones; but though I wince
I see what their opposite costs my sons.
They pay high for their gentle difference

From the mindless strength of competition;
Yet even now I am not convinced
That I was wrong (now that they rightly see
Weakness as tyranny, and have begun
To search themselves for true strength, desperately)
To hate unimagining ambition
Which says, "I'll be more," not, "Here's what I'll be."
A worse mistake I have regretted since:
My daughter was not taught priority
For her own work.
                Could I wash out those prints,
How, how could I now teach them differently?

6
Some women can see only males, and some
See only themselves, as if they too were male.
Both own the bitter equilibrium,
The base, hurt power of slaves. They are the frail
Employers of pity; they are dumb,
Cute, weak at will.
                My daughter did not learn
Those tricks. She neither flirts nor wails.
Generous & gentle, can she stand firm
Having found her own ground, or will she fail
(I've failed) to use her time and too late turn
To lay her claim? Can her young wisdom
Keep loving-kindness and yet rise to spurn
Unsuitable self-sacrifice?
                Now come
Two sisters to the pool where water burns.

7
The air above the sun-flamed pool is air
Changing into freshness. The two girls face
The subtle water. One sighs. Both stare
As if the split of mind from will were effaced

At last, by the freshening. They, laughing there,
Are the generation of the world. I see
Women may model a fresh human grace
That is not weak but deep for those set free
Of win & lose, and—present like this place—
Come from depth to breadth by pressing steadily.

A tall old woman whispers, de bon aire,
"Paradisa esta si." Is? Was? Not to me?
I'm confused. Her words startle everywhere.
Daughter, your paradisa is not; may be.

REPLAY, DOUBLED
This light is water in emerald ascent,
Old, holy; this water is where it lies
The font and vulva of the planet, brought
To light to open vision where the wise
Bend to the shoreline, cup their hands, and drink.
Though insight takes girls by sacring surprise
Their hands, if timid, touch its cold face
And know they are the sacred in disguise.
And even now I am not convinced
We would be wrong to worship who we are
As we come to the pool where water burns
Above a course that stone miles could not bar.
Grown from depth to breadth by pressing steadily,
We may stand human on our mother star.

A girl dips her foot in, holding her shoes,
Where all our history has come with praise.
Here her malfunction works in her like thought:
She can bear to be open and amazed
As the waters break. She may be afraid
Of the self-healed stillness that the pool displays,
Its face a peaceful force that intervenes
To soften stone; but it has turned her gaze

From weakness as tyranny, and begun
To model her. She's doffed her steep glass shoes
And the base, hurt power of slaves. She is frail.
She may go home glass-shod and deny this news
Of how to model a fresh human grace.
But she has been here. It is hers to choose.

GHOST WRITER

Irene on my tiny list of answers to despair
I star your name

But now I come to complain.
Lately, you only ghostwrite.
Able, serviceable, conscript
Papers on liverfluke or cattlebone,
Speeches on green research phrased
For a larynx not your own,
Replace in your portfolio the work
I think you were born to,
The personal words.
You have stopped writing those shapes
That leave calm people
              dizzy with listening to
              your truthful speakers
              say their human tunes.

Sensual, intellectual, acute to differentiate:
Sweet realist, you have always ghostwritten
What you can of what you cannot tolerate.
Strange to what sounds stupid
              you light-wristed
Transmute as you catch them
Our banal verbal moves into
        dazzles of juggled idea;
I am a bore but you are not bored; you
Fox me into surprises, for

You ghostwrite your friends too:
As you imagine how we act toward who we are
You better us;
You hear us

and, entirely pleasant
in earrings and a silk disguise,
you glance at the glass you hold,
you think, fast, speak,
smile,
swallow your drink,
And we see what you see we mean.
Then for the pleasures you give us
you thank us
So discreetly we accept your thanks.

Grace, as it dilates, effaces.
Is this how you become yourself?

You do become yourself.
Even your shy ankles are articulate of it;
Your hair no matter who cuts it is
Crisp as tulips and suits you; your
Voice, when you speak in it, is
Unmistakable, a rationale for words.
I catch
As it vanishes that chaste voice,
Behind the words, in years of pageants
You wrote for the children for holidays
—lost once played: daylilies, champagne, ephemera:
Bastille Day birthday high jinks,
a mime for a dancing giant,
Noah's arksong, solstice jokes,
now lost,
Matches written to be lit and lost—

You interrupt in your delicate French,
Its irony delicate, "Je regrette . . ."

Yes I regret your lost writing, the woodland
Dry its streams redirected, the stories
Left random, left unsaved,

Your sightseeing left unrecorded, lost,
Your language lent.
Yes yet
      no, I take back my complaint.

          I praise your Maygames
          your short always festivals
          their blaze-and-black fireworks,
          the confident gesture of them
          their formidable innocence.
The genius you modulate into helpful use thrives
          despite you,
          as the haunt of your lost lines
          improves your children into celebrants,
              your friends into imagined action,
              me into asking
If perhaps a woman
So rich is so free
She can
Sun-brilliant, sun-unseen,
Afford to keep
Herself like a secret, Irene,
And the secret, meekness
          unspeakable
          sanctity

OVERHEARD

1. LOGAN AIRPORT, BOSTON
"Kissed me hello & all that shit; I
Said to him are you
Seeing my sister?
Yes he said.
And she'd swore up and down
It was no such thing,
The picture of her was
     just a place
     looked
     like his backyard.
I got upset.
Seems like most people got to lie to me
Most of the time.
Don't want to break somebody's arm or head or that,
But I sure have got some news to break to her."

2. STUDENT UNION CAFETERIA
"That's not true, it don't alleviate nothing.'
What it alleviates
is me bustin my ass, for who
for my father
that's who, not even my mother
        that's another story,
for my father.
So since I got to bust my ass anyhow
I'd just as well move in with Mike
and let my
father
buy himself his own beer."

3. HIGH FALLS MARKET
"Nice little town it was;
Big city grew right on up out to
                    next door.
Ruined it. Ruined it.
From us to them
We still got 10–15 miles, rural
All rural.
Farmers swear it's going to last.
It won't last."

4. SENIOR CITIZENS' CENTER, QUEENS, NY
"They think it's better for kids to be brought up rich
they should ask my mother. Ask me. My father
big business man cigar and all, worked late worked
nights worked weekends, his big deals,
he didn't even know I was alive.
My mother used to dress me up for him, he never looked,
till I was 18 and wanted to get a job.
He had a fit. His
daughter had
a job, he said, to get a husband,
a Jewish boy, with a rich father business
man like him and a good job.
So I went and I got married to the poorest
Jewish boy I could find, brilliant,
no job, no head for business,
and poor is no good either.
He was just like my father, he
didn't know I was alive.
With him it wasn't business it was socialism."

THE DIFFÉRANCE: CHATOU-CROISSY

It was hard, but she was doing it,
Raising him well, the boy
Fathered on her by her mother's lover—
Buying his shoes in brand-name stores
Where fitting took time, keeping his teeth good.
Her skills were domestic, the knife
In her small hands all edge as it flashed
Rabbit flesh, parsley, leeks,
Into sizes she wanted.
When she could, she married a steady boy
Who'd never thought to get so fine a woman,
Who got on with her son,
Who even loved the boy though ashamed of him.

"Yes," she said, "he's of course the boss.
Whatever he says to do
I do, he loves to see me do it,
I never say a word. But now you're married,
I can tell you. Listen, let him be the boss,
Call him boss, all day,
Even in bed, do it his way,
Why not, ça ne coûte rien, and
He's got to sleep sometime:
That's your chance. Every night I wait till he snores,
Then I just lean my elbow into him until
He has to turn, a minute later I just lean
Again, he turns, you see? It's not for nothing
He's got pits of shadows all around his eyes,
The punk. You'll see, you can call him boss,
Boss all day, he'll eat it up,
Late at night, he never knows, you laugh."

LIVE MODEL

Who wouldn't rather paint than pose—
Modeling, you're an itch the artist
Doesn't want to scratch, at least
Not directly, and not yet.
You think, "At last, a man who knows
How bodies are metaphors!" (You're wrong.)

First time I posed for him he made
A gilded throne to sit me on
Crowned open-armed in a blue halfgown.
I sat his way, which was not one of mine
But stiff & breakable as glass,
Palestill, as if
With a rosetree up my spine.
We had to be speechless too,
Gut tight in a sacring thermal
Hush of love & art;
Even songs & poems
Were too mundane for me to quote
To ease our grand feelings
So I sat mute, as if
With a rosetree down my throat.

Now I breathe deep, I sit slack,
I've thrown the glass out, spit,
Evacuated bushels of roses.
I've got my old quick walk
& my big dirty voice back.

Why do I still sometimes sit
On what is unmistakably like a throne?
Why not. Bodies are metaphors,
And this one's my own.

HALF-LIFE: COPIES TO ALL CONCERNED

Gentlemen: how are you? Here things go well.
I write you after these many years to ask
If you have any news of all I lost
That I'd forwarded to you, insured, I'd thought,
First Class, on urgent demand, with a good
Guarantee (though that would be expired now).

What I miss is not you (as you do, now?)
But the girl I gave you. Did she do well,
That stern young person planning to be good,
Sure of her dress, her footing, her right to ask?
Lovers have half-life in each other's thought
Long after; is the mark she made quite lost?

Have you traces of her? That she got lost
I'd never guessed; but from what I hear now,
You never quite received her, though we thought
She knew more than the directions well
And would get by, skilled in what not to ask.
Were her efforts at lipstick any good?

Did she learn to tell bad eagerness from good?
If you do remember her, then she's not lost;
I've forgotten her so long, I must ask
(I didn't love her then as I might now)
What, for a while, told you you knew her well,
What live cry for her survives in your thought,

Who she was for you, what she meant, feared, thought.
She had trunks, jammed with what her love judged good;
Are they still somewhere, tagged & indexed well,
Or are they like my pictures of her lost?
I've saved what she left—stale or fragile now—
Latin books, laughs, wine, lists of what to do.

. . .

Should you have questions, do feel free to ask,
Given the always present tense of thought.
Though I know no time is as bad as now,
Recall her you—I could!—let him make good
The tale of that naked pure young fool, lost
Before I got a chance to know her well.

I should say, as well: beyond what I ask
Lies the you you lost, alive; in my thought
Still planning to be good. Redeem him now.

Now ask your thought for this lost good. Farewell.

UNABASHED

Unabashed
as some landscapes are
(a lakeshape, say,
lying and lifting
under a cupping sky)
     so angels are,
entire with each other,
their wonderful bodies
obedient, their strengths
interchanging—
     or so
we imagine them
hoping
by saying these things of them
to invent human love.

AS IS

Objects new to this place, I receive you.
It was I who sent for each of you.
The house of my mother is empty.
I have emptied it of all her things.
The house of my mother is sold with
All its trees and their usual tall music.
I have sold it to the stranger,
The architect with three young children.

Things of the house of my mother,
You are many. My house is
Poor compared to yours and hers.
My poor house welcomes you.
Come to rest here. Be at home. Please
Do not be frantic do not
Fly whistling up out of your places.
You, floor- and wall-coverings, be
Faithful in flatness; lie still;
Try. By light or by dark
There is no going back.
You, crystal bowls, electrical appliances,
Velvet chair and walnut chair,
You know your uses; I wish you well.
My mother instructed me in your behalf.
I have made room for you. Most of you
Knew me as a child; you can tell
We need not be afraid of each other.

And you, old hopes of the house of my mother,
Farewell.

NURSING: MOTHER

I

Tranquilized, she speaks or does not speak;
Immobilized, she goes to & fro invisibly.
The names of my children she recalls
Like a declension; my ex-husband is,
She thinks, the verb of a bad dream she had,
Irregular. When she listens,
What does she hear?
Kept in so long after school, it is her wits
That she, old traveler, sends wandering.
                    What joke
Will make her laugh? Doctor
Is she in pain? To her the nurse
Talks loud & slow as to a foreigner;
To whom have age and injury made
This most local woman alien?

Patient, she lies like a paradigm
Elaborate on her fenced high bed because
Her hip-bone snapped. Her doctor
Indicates his neat repair. I flinch
Before her sacredness.

From between those thighs
(Splashed in those days iridescent
With brighter-than-blood mercurochrome)
I thrust into sight thirsting for air
(So it must have been; so my children came;
So we commit by embodying it, woman to woman,
Our power: to set life free.
She set me free).

                    .   .   .

Long closed against me, now her flesh
Is a text I guess to read: Is
She in pain? My own flesh aches dumb
For a mummer's gift of touch
We might use to speak ourselves
Against this last fitful light
To mime the thirst we have.

2

To visit her I go among the graduates
Of ordinary discourse, where wryly
They command them who keep them.
Where they live is hot, rank, preserved,
Lion country.

In state among them Mother
Has her Lying-In as
Infant Empress whose otherness
Confuses the lions
And instructs them tame.

Where I dream she still walks domestic
In a peacock dress, bead-embroidered,
Aloof among my garden's raucous goats.
I dream her as blessing, with birds as gifts;
I dream her as the Tower's Priestess of cruel
Removal and Return, stepping in & out
At her will of her warm shadow, me.
I dream her serene, regent in her own
Diamonded mystery.

If I am hers she does not feel it.
The Empress Infant has no child.
She watches their antics as if her look
Kept the subject lions staked and tethered
Where they stalk. But suddenly,
"To see you," she says, "brightens me."

3

Here or dream, she is not at home. She
Can only come home to a boxroom brownstone
For breakfast on fried oysters & talk of the news
Of ships' arrivals in the Sunday *Tribune*
Between a man and woman who love her;
And even the walls of her homing are
Dust these forty years.

What she has kept of who she is
Is what the part calls for: a
Winsome dominance, speaking up
With a half-lost sense of audience; do
They tire of her she sleeps; do they smile
She is glad of it; what is she practicing?
Here on the flat of her bed the size
Of a flat box already ready in a factory.

Empress and Infant fear the toppling of the Tower.
She wishes the visitor were her mother, but
Trying it, saying, "Mom! How's Pop?"
Quickly adds, "Never mind. Never mind."

Today she said, "In the sun
Your hair has many colors,"
Quickly adding, "With these glasses
You got me, of course, I'm nearly blind."

LATE

for Marie Candee Birmingham, my mother

1

Dark on a bright day, fear of you is two-poled,
Longing its opposite. Who were we?
What for? dreaming, I haunt you unconsoled.

Rewarded as I force thought outward, I see
A warbler, a Myrtle, marked by coin-gold—
I feel lucky, as if I'd passed a test,
And try my luck, to face the misery
Of loss on loss, find us, and give us rest.
Once we birdwatched, eyeing shrub & tree
For the luck beyond words that was our quest;
Your rings flashing, you showed me day-holed
Owls, marsh blackbirds on red wings, the crest
Kingfishers bear. Mother, dreams are too cold
To eye the dark woodland of your bequest.

2

To eye the dark woodland of your bequest
I wear the fire of diamond on my hand,
Flawed extravagance of your first love expressed
In a many-faceted engagement band.
Recklessly cut with the blaze I invest
In my dazzling flaws, careless of weight,
The fiery cast of mind that I love planned
To sacrifice carat-points for this bright state.
It is yours still, and I go talismanned
By you to find you, though I'm lost & late.
You left this for me; ringed I go dressed
To mother us, mother, to isolate
And name the flight of what, mouth to rich breast,
We meant while we were together to create.

3

We meant while we were together to create
A larger permanence, as lovers do,
Of perfecting selves: I would imitate
By my perfections, yours; I would love you
As you me, each to the other a gate
Opening on intimate gardens and
Amiable there. Mother you were new
At it but when you looped us in the bands
Of clover hope to be each other's due,
The hope at least lasted; here I still stand
Full of the verb you had to predicate.
Though you as subject now are contraband
Half hidden, half disguised to intimidate,
I recognize your diamond on my hand.

4

I recognize your diamond on my hand
As the imagined world where we were whole.
Now among boxed boxes, pine roots, & Queens sand,
You have changed places with this bit of coal,
Dark to light, light to dark. To understand
The dark your child never was afraid of
I go lightless sightless birdless mole
In the dark which is half what words are made of;
I enter the dark poems memories control,
Their dark love efficient under day love.
Down I go down through the oldest unscanned
Scapes of mind to skim the dim parade
Of images long neglected lost or banned,
To root for the you I have not betrayed.

5

To root for the you I have not betrayed
I hunt the ovenbird we never found—
Or guessed we'd found when something leafbrown strayed
Under the trees where soft leaves lay year round.

When you'd said, "Hush," and we'd obeyed (obeyed
Lifelong too long) "Tea/cher!" we heard; the shy
Bird spoke itself, "Tea/cher!" from the dim ground
The call came plain enough to recognize
And we went out following the sound.
It went before us in the dusk; its cries
Go before me now, swerve & dip in shade
Woman daughter bird teacher teach me. Skies
Boughs brush tufts; blind I have lost where we played
All trust in love, to the dark of your disguise.

6
Trust in love lost to the dark of your disguise,
I forget if I loved you; I forget
If, when I failed, you requisitioned lies;
Did we make believe we saw the bird, and set
On my lifelong list what my long life denies:
That we found what we wanted side by side?

But I did see you bird I see you yet
Your live glance glinting from leafdust; you hide
Calling, colorless, your brief alphabet
Sharp. Wait, wait for me. Flash past, dusty bride,
Stand safe, rosefooted, before my finite eyes.
Sing, undeafen me. Bird be identified.
Speak yourself. I dread love that mystifies.
Say we wanted what we found side by side.

7
I say I wanted what I found at your side.
("Is that your mother?" yes. "But she's a tea/
cher." Yes. I see that.) Reading, sunned, outside,
I see your lit hand on the page, spirea
Shaking light on us; from your ring I see slide
A sun, showering its planets across skies
Of words making, as you read or I or we,
A cosmos, ours. Its permanence still defies

The dark, in sparkles on this page; fiery,
It makes its statement clear: light multiplies.
No matter on whose flawed hand what jewel rides
Or who quickens to what bird with jeweled eyes,
The light of the planet is amplified.
Bird your life is diamond and amplifies.

REPLAY
The luck beyond birds that was our quest
I find in you. Although I'm lost & late
Our hope at least lasted; here I still stand
In your dark love, efficient under day love;
It goes before me in the dark, its cries
Sharp. Wait, wait for me. Flash past, dusty bride.
Make your statement clear: light multiplies.

Hommages

HOMMAGES À CHARLES PERRAULT

Once there was a king the old man writing
his heart out wrote who had a daughter
and whose dearest wife was dead.
Now this princess ("not yet fifteen") was
beautiful comme le jour
et le petit jour as the day
as the dawn of day is beautiful.

Charles aging elegant and grand
absolute owner of several styles
shut over his own verse book
declined many desirable invitations
rose early, mornings, and went walking among new
statues down the hazegreen vistas spry with birds
court cats and children playing in the royal
pleasure gardens of the Tuileries.
Statues children creatures presences
moved around him softly made him move
around and down around the riverhaze spring vistas
turning in a hushing lilt of echoes
soundless over the ordered grounds
among shy welcome whisperings and laughing cries.

They saw him home, came in, and stayed
liminal, watching among the hours of the afternoon,
until he sat and wrote to net
in his steady tall fine script
shimmering young girls who came alive, in flower-
embroidered gowns, jewel-crowned, attended,
or in loose silks, gone flower-gathering.

The old man dredged. The murexed fables
fish-flashed up, a catch that had enchanted once

an upon-a-time petit Charlot
when his nurse or rarely mother
scared and satisfied him so.

He wrote, to satisfy his presences,
for every era rank and age of man
  himself especially
  bonhomme bon père bon mari
  bon bourgeois de Paris
(except for sanitary wives whose
germless infants sicken easily,
except for those whose sanitary
lives lack love enough to be afraid
who harbor what they must deny
gnomes witches ogres wicked
second marriages).

Lucid, addressed by secrets and slight presences,
hiding them with light, he addressed himself to these . . .
Red-wristed girls in from Nancy and St.-Lô
alone, indoors, in the evening with only
another woman's brats to comfort and take
comfort from, poor driven maids, could climb
to their cold attics glowing, having
spelled out how high poor driven maids may go
telling aloud the bedtime tales of the Perrault.

Young women of the great families, even
those who practiced intelligence, became
the picture of mothering, his "Histoires
ou contes" in hand, awaiting the occasional
ceremony of the children's visit.
Noble ears heard their own diamond-cut
-diamond world in that perfectly
acceptable noble prose hearing, really,
tunes neglected hearts like theirs
might dance a measure of, crying on dear wishes,

imaginary innocence, undistracted limbs,
and a sleep reflecting petals
fast among the slowly opening
roses of forever-after love.

He intended, too, the smiles over small heads at his wit, that
famous in its day had all Paris laugh as Perrault saw fit;
he intended to have the smilers' sleeping bravest longings
stirring to be spoken of, unsmiling, under it.
"What's your cause, old man?"
      "Myself. And I have pled it well."
Innocent of causes, his fancies freed him too;
a costly freedom, even in an age of skilled extravagance
a brilliant and abandoned buy. The discipline of years
held good: only a third of his heroes are hideous
 : splayed, humped Ricky, and the Beast, and how
splendor of person came upon them
being loved by heroines not yet fifteen

(and what Bluebeard, unloved, became)

how all advisors but the ugly lover fail
(what had Bluebeard been, obeyed?)

and how royal love-matches reward
love that can take pity and keep faith.

But children, listening
hear with children's passionate hearing
the sounds of the stories and wait to take
the moment when the known voice makes
a shape and it's the magic word
            Is it the stained
found key to Bluebeard's nest, or the leggy
wolf's big appetite, or the ass who crapped out
little piles of gold in coins,
is it all the lovely girls "not yet fifteen"?

It is death and gaming, quick-come sighs of joy,
now unmerited, now earned by pluck propriety or love;
extempore, eternal, terrible, and all quite true.

Confirming children's knowledge of the world,
he yet allows them hope.
He gives them, see, quiet and clearly
surrounded by sun in a radiance of air
among small grasses pied with flowers
a few flower stalks in her hands
the girl who is glory and gold
simply, where she stands.
       He also gives
infinite permissions to be a child
and all the persons children are;
even the well-known secret witch must leave
her cave of shadows and come out
wearing a name it's safe to say aloud
to meet the well-known secret powerful
godmother gifted and gifting with her wand.
It is ourselves we make as he makes us believe.

Nights of nightmares ripen into dreams; splintery
facts round out into shapes of stories for
children moving toward their truth, advancing
constant and glorious on the rich real world
as they courageous under the covers keep
growing up, sleep by troubled sleep.

GRAND MOTHER TO MIRANDA

for Muriel Rukeyser, who says,
"I'd rather be live Muriel than dead Ariel."

As grace to wit is courage to Muriel;
Her song says though its voices are various,
"There is no truth that is not usable."

The drawn line, the equation, the syllable
Each tells her truths equally curious;
As grace to wit is wisdom to Muriel.

In strike or stroke, tragic or comical,
Her sight unblinds us to what's serious:
There is no dream that is not usable.

Model & mother, her mind makes visible
The great world she claims as home for us;
As grace to wit is justice to Muriel.

From *Flight* to *Gates* her hope grows more radical;
It shows us search is never impious
And there is no growth that is not usable.

Intimate of Caliban as of Ariel
Her voice improves the gentle & the furious;
As grace to wit is woman to Muriel:
There is no truth that is not usable.

OF CERTAIN STUDENTS

Once, teachers were giants of the numinous
—Plato, Plotinus, Porphyry, Iamblichus—
Whose sandaled academies trod holily on air;
I praise them but (in class) am not envious.
Ritual can't spin up out of the likes of us;
We're safe.
      Yet we, not even friends, do exchange
Fierce energies. Playing at change,
We do change. Sometimes, you gesture and
From off your hands blades of light flash.

Sometimes in your absences
I turn you into lists of things
To do, and do them.

Often in your presences
I make lists, in the thinlooped snares
That language casts, of things I ought to say
(And you could sing them)
Great things—and some days your tongues
Are so quick they spring them.

FOR JOHN KEATS
on the sense of his biography

Cold,
John Keats coughs and spits blood.
                    And in the space
between the meaning and the dream, still does.
It spoke. He heard it, the bright arterial word.
Dying, he tried to exchange himself for verbal
closure of that space. Trying, having sealed
his present for us, he died.

Though many brutal English winters since
have struck the wet heath cold through
                    the lowest layers of its stone
& as many May weeks sunsteamed it into
a carpet thick with soft
                    explosions of short flowers,
to praise Keats's presence now helps me.

When he said he wanted to write successfully
Keats meant commercially, planned to arrange
a marriage of his gift with Byronic
                    cash & fame,
planned to dazzle his girl some day with diamonds
replacing amethysts. Through that promising
dream (trying for audience, shaping his skills)
the spring sun shone when friends and the woman
presented him with promises.
He became the clement season he needed,
plenteous in language
as in primrose the garden was, he breathing
between the cut grass and the plum
tree as if his were the coming
unbudding of summer, for a while.
Words rushed for him toward ripening

and, like full summer in the plums,
flushed in the shaping crystal of his glass;
their long light became the Keats we summer in.
The answer to winter is such saved time.
It is how he keeps us warm.

He had further to go, though; soon
the spot flew vivid from his throat
onto the linen pillowcover
and, bowered in by cotton fields of flowered lawn,
he began the life of what it is to die.
With riches, diamonds, and his darling girl
                    a bankrupt fantasy,
close to the comfort of his narrowing bed,
he brided his burden, married
his person to his voice. Mouth on mouth
lost in each other they enclosed
the soundless now of his necessity,
making love present gratuitously
                    as the pulse & tune, in what he wrote, of
                    what he did not write: his history,
until one day
the birds fell silent for
the singing of the tree.

Though nothing lives that does not die,
nothing dies that does not live.
The price of death is life.
The doctor in him died to find that out;
the lover in him died
                    to shine for us
on the leafy life we bear to our exchange with death.

Full of blood or words his mouth
lifted up the shape of the present tense.
That present is the secret poets dare not keep
or tell. It makes them mind. It makes them speak.

Some of them stuff the script of their saying
behind the books on a shelf or under
the other papers in the drawer, startled
if caught making audible the
name tuned beyond union or disunion,
ashamed to have let the tenor of the now
escape upon the loud wind script can go cold in.

As leaf and branch speak flight and water
Keats both keeps and speaks the secret,
quieting that fear
for the rest of us. When
he happened to his writing,
his future disappeared.

I sit outside his Hampstead house & estimate
the age of the mulberry tree.
They say it was old in his time.
It looks young to me.

OUR LADY

for Marilyn Hacker

The thing about you, Mary, thank you,
is that you are grounded where we are
when we are trying to do well;
your truth is not conciliar
but ours and actual.
You are not Bona Dea but Bona
certainly, bona femina,
mulier, woman, wanted, insulted,
a woman like us, like me
though enshrined in seacliffs,
high places, caves, deep cathedrals,
and wherever fresh water springs or falls.
You are known
for nothing
      but that you had free will
      and that once gravida
you proved that birth, perceiving
a new perceiving point, renews;
you proved
women may suffer but do not die
of solitude work love or loss.
When all you had was what you lent,
you sang, you sang.
I tell the strong poet this & she smiles,
your smile (joy undifferentiated
in the speed of assent)

FOR A SEASON

We saw we had few words to exchange when two by two
By two over our heads birds like omens flew
Making space between us dangerous.

    Glances can be truthful; this I learned
    When with your sharp breath the time turned
    Very sharp and felicitous.

And truth is unknowable. Who knows
How far to where the loving goes
When its action makes free of us?

    Generously we lay together
    Under the Irish weather.
    It was summer due to us.

ON THE COUNTRY SLEEP OF SUSANNE K. LANGER

Though she lives there as the wood's
human creature, "carrying water,"
though in her sound shoes she is native to it,
the land even the boundary river
    even when she sleeps
centers about her;
      centered it tenders
its myriad finalities
sunning them
in her energy of shaped ideas.

Focus of the forest focus
of the continent's intelligence
minded in the lucent
patience of her appetite
Susanne K. Langer doctor
thankless for wisdom's sake
entertains giant
ghosts, ours & her own; introduces
ideas to each other, reconciles
caves & skyscrapers of selves,
to become a familiar
of where the spirit lives
until even her sleep
is contemplative.

As beginning & end of that act she informs
her forest house.
To watch her in the high wood the night
is willing to be dark.
Beside her raised bed are pencils, yellow,
one in a mottled notebook keeping
her place. Between earth

and elsewhere,
wisewoman, sleeping,
she keeps her place.

Tabled on upstate clifftop
bedrock New York Susanne is lifted up

and though about her the moonlight were
just moonlight,

she lies generic inside
the steep hush of the grove,
earthwoman, offered as
a symptom of our health through
treecrowns & expanding atmosphere to
the skies.

In so focal a biography such sleep
recalls the cast of sacrifice.

LULLABY

Sleep now, hush my
fragile beast,
fed new child, sleep.
Look at you, soft,
life locked to you
safe in your fist;
no light enters yet
like flowers you retain
all the light there is
blotted up like a stain.
Even at dusk you lie,
though this room looks east,
luminous in it; the shadows
stoop so you are centered
as you leach from the air
the last of the light
to show you as holy
as you are fair.
Sleep now. There there.
Good night.

ANTENNAE

Though I like to recline or lie
like the horizon in contact, Dame Kind,
flat out for you as I will more
closely one day be,
I get up when you turn to the light
and stand what I call tall.
Small
my feet flat to their task
at least one always touching you,
my head stuck out further
than my feet by what
I call an important distance,
an oracular one (these differences
of distance between head & feet
being what there is of me),

I look around at us your short
antennae, little bristles, erect if
crookedly so, mobile—
and I admire our stance.
We are brave our heads
sticking out kangarooed
in your generous pocket;
I admire our power to imagine you,
our plots to lighten your burden & lift
ourselves to your beyondness, outside
the nourishment of air.

I admire the tenuous delight feet
take toward you in flatness,
admire what of your voice we have
that keeps speaking you, setting
waves of complicating sound surging

with daring over your continents,
while my bones
hold my significant
upright & interested,
for part of each day,
for decades of years.

A THIRD THANK-YOU LETTER
for the gift of the Vert-Galant

The Seine and the sky refract each other's rain.

Unrefracting, I
lost June looking for you.

Every river needs an island
to underline its wetness with
that surge of green plume
every island needs.

And here, among the green where
the curve of the river ramparts retains
the river in stone, and the curves in pencil
retain the pulse of these words,
you are.

It is after all late spring: I write
"You are here, after all."
For the rest of the morning
I do not need to remember
anything; for the rest of the day
there is the morning to remember;
I think we remember it together.

The blunt barge nose slowly shows
the middle bridge arch has been chosen, and
glides under; behind
the long flat of it, the person with
bright mind in the less bright white
wheelhouse looks down over coal-
heaps at Vert-Galant, glances with
your brightness,
waves and grins
above the integrating water.

. . .

In the July mist I welcome you.

You offer me the river, grey
as the sky but glaucous like Homer and
olive leaves or like puddles of oil paint
cupping dark green & pulsing silver
in every direction.

Babbling, I've missed you.
In St.-Sévérin I did not see the pillar I
talked about though it leapt up like
you for us, living, the line emerging
from the stone in three dimensions yet
linear therefore envisioned and springing
clear as mind from living brain.
I am in fact usually
much too busy to look for you.
No wonder I catch cold. The casual
river does better, always watching the sky.

Opposite, along the outer thigh of the given river,
some trees are missing from the row, plane trees
gone to lighten traffic where the toy
cars speed toward Notre Dame (you
are, in them, less reflected than you are,
my brightness, by the river
though their metal winks for you boldly). Today

the river is what you have given me,
and the locust the willows the chestnut
of the small in-position park, emerging head-down
from the river's undulant pelvic floor,
lying along the modular inner thighs of the river
new green to encourage the signals
of new lovers, games of new children, new
farewells of old voyagers.
                    Because I have been here

watching and in place for one hour
you have come flooding back to me
bearing ransom. Awash with that limpid
identity, I take you in. All islands are
always being born; each needs
a like inhabitant, interacting, riverborne:
here I am, just down from the palace of justice
greening, crowning, new at the feet of Notre Dame,
assuming your welcome
and welcoming you
gratefully

grown to want
what I have
and to have
what I want
where I want
what I have
to be

Discovery

DISCOVERY

Though I sit here alone I
am smiling and
realize why as I find
that the answer (to my own
old poser of who will be
my magna mater) is clear;
I can even understand
her invisibility
for she, the grand
mother (I've always needed)
    is surely here
    too close to see
    for I am she.
Laughing she explains nothing.

My life is given back to me.

For we survived seedtime
(some seeds pop their pods and jump away;
some eased out of clumps by gold birds
float off, alight, and again drift;
some, deer after drinking drop
near a pleasant stream) we
survived and the winter
was kind to the seed
and now the winter has lifted;
I leave the season of need.

Daughter gone to lover of daughter,
sons to lovers of sons, all
have gone from me readily
with the extended almost soundless leap
of trust in genital clemency.

Left to myself I discover
that what had to spring together
has sprung together and the fields
are beds of blossoming,
the hollow meadows fill
again with blossoming.

Blessing the gardeners I do not doubt
the benefits the blessing yields
as daily less anxiously
I walk out among them
or windsoft beyond them
unheard unheeded
not lost not needed
reaching invisibly
for what is great yet proper to me
and cannot but mother me:
unconsidered liberty.

FIELD OF VISION:
A MAP FOR A MIDDLE-AGED WOMAN

I

  The wind changes; I slept in it
Like a stone awash at the bottom of the stream.
With the sun, the mist and I rise.
  I fall upward to wake outside
  The numbered myths of measure
  Into real time.
  I fall awake beyond
  The distancing myths of memory
  Blinking to see
  Measurelessly.
Mortal eyes, mine, seeing almost
A hemisphere at a time, here see
It is late summer, a shimmering.

At my foot, flat up to face the sparse
Light of the clifftop orchard, grow
Furred, rounded (feel!) leaves
In the lee of a sitting stone; overhead
Among old boughs a few apples gleam.

I have never seen anything like it.
It is lonely (lone in likeness, singular),
Lovely (that is, like love). Orphan,
I know no other seasons; unlicensed,
I am not a country person; what I see
Is that nothing real happens twice.
Twice, nothing happens. Grasshoppers' angles
Differ; each jump of theirs links known to new.
My childhood Flying Dutchmen are no clue to these.
Memory's to think with, not daydream absently—
It should be like light on leaping, rain on water,
To make the mind run richer, a brilliance
Merging emerging in the shimmering interchange.

。　。　。

Naming the four points of their land, East first,
The old Celts stood still, then spun to name as fifth
The unity of the four, finite yet mobile,
The space of authority, their sacred place.
In our cooler categories we observe
Six locatives looking left, right,
Up, down, fore, aft: Pines, appletrees,
Blue space through branches, a subtle hill,
Earth grassed & flowering, a cliffedge
Treed. Six. Three pairs. And?
            and I
            am here:
            I name a
            center a
            point of view place,
            fluid;
            as two-handed I go
            on the ground among trees
            toward trees, under the sun,
            away from the hill.
This seventh this perceiving
Point may or may not be
Perceived. I feel perceived,
Perhaps as part of my perceiver,
Where I stand sniffing the morning wind
Determined to take my time, to make it clear,
And—maybe—to conceive of memory.

2
It's hard work.
I can't just abandon the treasure and
Rubble of my inner cities that extend
Beyond where memory gone dim
Is a lens in mist
That by distortion lies.
It won't dissolve. It greys the air with twists

Of ghosts: vain accusers, or lovers, or the dead,
Or at best, echoes, unfair to their vivid origins.

I shout attack
Through the spun-glass atmosphere:
Paris I have never walked your rings; what's
A nightingale? Dowth never have I entertained
Your populous earthwork beyond the fish-inscript
Lintel down the dry passage
At the bottom of the well.
I never met anyone
At the top of the stairs on Christopher Street.

Poems, rock stars, I've never caught
Your new acts on the festival circuit of languages
I never patched light-shows for.
Words, tuned to your own meanings, amps off,
Don't parade in a razzma of overtones
Across the acoustic field
Between me and whatever whispers here.
Lover,
Hard haunched, I have never
Worked trapeze with you
(Or you, lion-maned,
Or you, brandy-splashed, or)

If in strong sun I shout and
The false protective lens or mist
Burns off, if I do without them,
Originals revive.
Daughter, sons, born
Out of the pulsing channel of me,
You consented, each to your own acts,
When at the last breathless moment
You turned your face away from mine
And shouldered, springing, into life
Breathing your lonely breathing

That is like love.
I now disenchant
The frozen totems of your names.
I bid the powerful mystery
That shrouds your names and shrouds
Other loved names of great power over me,
Evaporate. My ears,
That have listened for you
As you no longer are,
Want a hush now and the new.

3
Too bad I can't juggle up a rite of departure
With classic control & in traditional costume
But I have no stage directions.
To be quit I must pay off the worst of you
Vulgarly
      or you'll come on tour with me
By mistake or for blackmail. You ghosts,
Reluctant to go, claim me by false shame:
          shame of lies,
Shame of turning my head lazily away,
Shame of wishing debts paid, owed letters mailed,
Silly shame of missed cues, shame of grief
In brutal places I did not change;
The guilt is mine and I dismiss you;
You are ugly and powerful with sorrow

    sorrow sorrow
    child of comparisons

How will I live without the shaming sorrow
I have dwarfed in a body of selfishness?
So far so good, I walk solid
In a daylight field of vision.
Though the woman walking is
Only me I am central among flashing

Differences (leaves like needles, leaves
That touch like fingers, leaves like islands,
The thousand ingenious ways of being green)
I can watch accurately and see
The little less than an eyelid difference
Between seeing in or out, diminish
Among the shimmering.

4
A maple has thrust roots back in among the rock
Half down the cliff I'm on top of (I am not
A city person). Its leaves wall an aerial
Tunnel that opens into a changing frame for
A mist, maybe off sunned water, rising;
Beyond it lie the shapes
Of a woodland, a pasture, someone's
                                    someone else's.
Barkbrown, scuppering in short arcs, bug catcher,
Bird, I am new here: who are you?
No bird is alien when every wing is strange.
In the newness of strangeness what flights
I may contain I can't guess. Without guidebook,
Unrehearsed, where I climb,
Each shape to take the air
Is the only; all are first;
None last.
I can tell the difference.

Apples sweet with old storms,
Old fires of sun, tasty, eaten
In extreme hunger—I exchange
Their old life for mine.
For ripe fruit
Thank the tree;
And I will yet thank me, if
Splotched still with dried time
I can be washed unstiff of history,

If inside the outside of me
Is me.

Good-by apples; grow, grow,
Other travelers' guts will welcome
Your fiery sugars
                    not I, not again;
Abandoning the orchard I quit claim
To satisfaction changed, celled, stored
In the tight-skinned shapes of time fulfilled.

Down in the stream I sandscrub off the camouflage
Loonlight, sunspots, troublers of vision,
Moonstains of schedules, the last
Stiff, eclectic freckles, until
I can't contract for anything.

MAUVE

Last night a few beads or half-
moon spots in the grass
prophesied this shining. Reflections wink
on leaf and blade that the wind tips;
the glint of their fresh life is soft.
It is the moment of spring mauve
when certain tulips, ajuga,
and species bleeding-heart offer together,
blued down from frank pink, their
cups spikes and two-centered
flimsy bells. They rise a little
above the new green, and tilt
in the water-sounding air
full of lilac fall.

It could be any year of the last fifty
that I move among them (we never lose
our first lilacs; I stir here
and up absent avenues
layers of that smell drift,
under this smell, magnetic) as if
as once I were ignorant
not of doing
but of knowing
about having to.

ADVICE: AD HAEREDITATES, I

The water:
    I pour it
    with care
into these seven jars for
you seven,
sacred voyagers
soon to be launched.
    One of you will
one day need it;
I have seen signs
    in your faces; one
    will need it.
Each of you is
I judge able to need it.

I pray this good water
be to your hand in time of want.

I look into your faces o
my God my children!
    (yes, such talk, the least-
    considered catch of the heart,
    makes pagans guess false worship.
    Well, not their fault; they do not
    know there is one difference
    language does not make.)

You suppose, my seven, that you too
are pagan, my lovely children. When
your turn calls, you will
        lose the lift of doubt.
               · · ·

You are setting out now.
I may not be here when you
        come back. Two or three
may find me still around
or find me elsewhere,
on the road or in
grandbabies' faces; sooner or later,
however, we meet again.

You have a taste of the water,
        coronal, in the small
        vials you always carry.
In case you need it, in case
you've half forgotten the true
flavor when someone wants to
sell you lots of wetness
and you need something sustaining,
        or in case
dreaming you dream you are no longer
refreshed by thinking of drinking it—
well, my children, in any such
great emergency
        go ahead,
        break the vial open,
drink your drop, you
won't be able to forget the flavor, then.
Being grown up, having
chosen it and tasted it again,
you may ache
for all—yourself too—who are
usually thirsty but
you won't be unsure of it;
no one ever is, or has been in my
time or my mother's either.

For there is never as much water
available to share or store as we'd like,

never. Nor do most of us manage
to give enough time to locating
new springs and keeping
old sorts of jars, vials, bottles
both safe and accessible. I hear
they do it better, in some places
nowadays; they have special processes.
Probably, voyaging, you'll learn
improvements in methods I haven't
dreamed of. That's progress. For instance,
one way my mother didn't know, I learned
on a voyage of my own: Be dry be as dry
with yourself as you can, so as to
absorb what you need in passing
from the ground or right from the air.
It can happen. Though you miss
the shocking joy of taste,
it will do you its good anyway.

Now, I must say that I have not
tried hard enough, left you enough
except for emergencies, even in quantity. That's
not the worst though: I haven't foreseen
every emergency. There too
I did not do as well as I was able.
        But you will forgive me,
those of you anyway who never face
emergency I failed to foresee.
        The one who does meet it
head-on will not forgive me
        unless
        maybe
        after.
When you separate, try
to remember to say
(at least! to yourself)
some little

ceremonious
good-by;
take leave
of each other
gracefully.
It saves agony later
when you meet again.
The old ceremony,
the effort you gave it, will
stir your memory warmly,
children.

I've often heard,
"The greater the quantity
the less the thirst in & around you,"
therefore these jars—though
I believe those who say
one drop can suffice
for a lifetime, and no lifetime
lacks that drop. Some disagree;
you'll see for yourselves.

What we know for certain
is that this is water
—mine to give you
what I may of it—
that nothing
can spoil.

ADVICE: AD HAEREDITATES, II

I
What it is to fall
    (down through the high
    terror of a world gone all
    one Midas color, gold, and I
    deaf to every voice but one)
in love, and the joy of that, I recall.

While I praise the incomparable
attitudes, the touching disguises,
the notice desire takes, intimate as sun,
of the beloved as it day by day devises
bars of delicate jealous reasons for
the prison of the univocal,
           I recall
the failures that follow on
being everything to anyone,
& the excuses for failure that collect to rise
like fog before love-stricken eyes
to dim love's simpler cruelties:
    dinners missed, work abandoned,
    friends' addresses lost, and all
    so that one more deaf gamble
    for ecstasy eternal
    might go down—
and I long
to make a joke of my great ignorance
and yours, to say that as a way
of learning other human beings are
alive, such comic ordinary deafness may
be the only way, and harmless, so long
as lovers keep in mind the chance or hope
of hearing universal song.

For hearing may be restored:
in autumn in America where
we are the migrants there are
never nightingales but now, if there were,
I'd be able to hear them.

2

To be able to hear again is to begin to be
among other persons, intimately free.
If you can hear your lover without fear, hear
friends and value that, listen even to blood
relations you trust as couriers, carriers,
you will—entertaining such harmony—
learn it is not bleak it is like music and
imagining music, to be out of love.
It is the next instrument to smile to be
first nowhere
in no heart first,
never deaf (to every voice but one),
first on no list of invitations,
first to the decency of no enterprise.
You will know
should the purser shriek Fire, the sirens
confirm him, the ship burn, everyone
you included would first rather
save someone other than you.
You will like to become
a person nobody would destroy
or die to rescue, to be
useful, yes tuneful, but expendable;
as loss, to be small loss
so that those bereaved of you would care
(as is good for everyone, to care)
might grieve, might cry out once remembering
on waking some small characterizing thing
but no more than might be good for them.

.　.　.

To imagine this music
choose as instrument something small
(finger bells would do)
so most quartets can form
without you; practice singing
in chorus, joyfully, and learn
to listen as you sing.

3
Although I have chosen it or
it has chosen me,
I'm still afraid to claim
I can keep such tunes harmoniously—
afraid that when in the night the ship
cracking & flaming between
two unsustaining darks
is wrecked
I will still long to rush to place
my chosen one safe in the last lifeboat letting
the rest shriek unheard & go down if need be.
That fear is why
random & ambient,
waiting for more
than the budding of wisdom,
waiting for its fruit & fruitful core,
which may surprise me at the core,
I stay ashore.

Though in my many-voiced harbor city
there are no nightingales, I take
pleasure in the signals starlings make,
in the definite lessons
they know in their hollow bones
how to give their successors: "Cats
kill us," & "Squirrels raid our nests,"
they can say with an eternal starling
agreement; they say, "We eat this grain,"

"We can kill other fledglings for food,"
"We bank to turn," consistently.

If I envy them it's for your sake,
to excuse the confusion, children,
of the way these lines break
like boys' voices under my uncertain
unstarling working definition of the human
music. For the wingless human mind
no form of instruction is modular,
& most true words lie, before
they can be cut in stone.
Of course you know all this already, know
your thoughts are secret as your bones,
no matter how well you learn a beloved,
how much you work to be learned, or
how deaf you walk within desired joy;
your skin is a limit all your own.

Thanks to the admitting ear
we learn to hear as we begin to sing
until (shaking our bells) we have grown
to overhear love as it mingles its voices,
each accidental voice (ours too) essential
and original, a signal for alone.

ADVICE: AD HAEREDITATES, III

I drop in on you; we all encircle
one table again, & I realize
for the old kinds of listening between us
it is at last too late.
Now I don't like to talk to
you my darlings, as darlings,
though I still have all our history to say.
I carry its weight heavy as infant eyelids
and as secret, untransferable.
I carry packs of albums, films, old toys,
first-grade schoolbags, elixirs healthful
or fatal, none false, all out of date.

My baggage belongs to you, yours to lose or store,
mine to get rid of and walk the lighter for;
but I can't just hand it over anymore.
I must let it go. Will you find it? you may.
(All mistakes are only temporary anyway.)
Magic is only a language women once
invented for mute men; you are not mute;
so these things of words I could have crooned or droned
when we were wordless prophets of your world
I let drift away as we sit here, adult,
and otherwise articulate.

What matters is not what they are—all common stuff—
but what they assert of their direction; they came
aimed from where you were once to where I was,
& since we are nowhere near there now
they drop into their proper orbit
not lost but declining; they
spiral and will (drawn into gravity
through the silence of mine to the center of your
memory) fall to rendezvous, come home.

A PROPRIETY

Trees are the rich man's
flowers or the giant's
              or the idler's;
they stand compatible in kinds in
the landscape—locust fringing pine—
like slow bouquets
composed by infants to be
enjoyed by the very old,
        wild bouquets assembled in
        selecting seasons of patience
                    endurance
                    eventual
        impatient failure to endure.

Constellations are gatherings
for those older
vaster or idler still or
for children and the landless
        who can have
        no space to imagine as earth
        of their own and garden in—
and so inherit all the sky.

ANTI-ROMANTIC

I explain ontology, mathematics, theophily,
Symbolic & Aristotelean logic, says the tree.

I demonstrate perspective's & proportion's ways.
I elucidate even greyness by my greys & greys & greys.

Gravity's laws, the four dimensions, Sapphic imagery,
Come from contemplating me,
Says the tree.

I rightly exhibit the functions of earth & air:
Look up at & through my branches, leaved budded or bare
Laid lustrous in their degrees against infinity,
& your seeing relates you to all of space, through me.
Here's aesthetics, too. No sight's nearer to perfectly fair.
I am mediate and immediate, says the tree.

I am variable, exquisite, tough,
Even useful; I am subtle; all this is enough.
I don't want to be a temple, says the tree,
But if you don't behave, I will be.

HARDSHIPS OF THE ORDINARY ASTRONOMER

On summer nights when after much sun
the temperate flesh is ready to lie out
in the meadow & study, all the wide high
air's awash and flickering;
stars crowd in thickets; they brush in,
brush out of sight, swamping
the map in mind.

This winter night when feet & face
long to navigate closely the radial
ambience of stove,
the heavy cold
declaims the stars' courses.
They stand out in the glass and propose
their formations, which advance engraved,
each distance visible, for those with
shelter and strong instruments.
Short of sun, we can't face the cold
long enough to learn
if other suns can warm.

Our sun we glory in. It clothes
& clocks us obedient to what
we can afford to admit of light.
It hides us from the galaxies, and them,
for a while, from our sight;
its dark hides us daily
though apparent dark has passed.
Even if aloft, where we drift
immersed in sunwash,
we do not imagine
under how much human night
our day is cast.

. . .

Drawn
—though confused by our longing—
to acclimatize our vision to what
we think are night skies,
we choose coordinates, set up
the tripod, save up for the lens.
We study charts with a pleasure
made modest by knowing
whatever our algebra aims at,
it is ourselves we measure.

Yet it is the personal
that links us body to body
in the gigantic intercourse, fugal
among the spheres. We are in person those
who, though our sun's dark interferes,
are drawn and stare and listen
to catch tremendous vestiges.
Our hands,
where the capacity inheres, record
what we have caught; our eyes,
able to, read what other hands report.

Though we suppose
that personal time comes
close as sleep to silence
while the faithful heart knocks softly in its cage,
and suppose that kept time is louder though
it only ticks or hums
              according to our pleasure,
we know we are children in what we suppose,
having no ear or other acoustical
devices nor any lens or
vehicle that can come

anywhere near there where the principal
brilliance linking the galaxies
incorporates unmediated

      our mortal loud
flutes, bass fiddles, drums.

NATIVE SPEAKER

Half an hour till my first class,
Student Union cafeteria, the *Times*,
a cup of coffee at an orange table
between the artificial & the window light,
good mornings, bad news; editorials
about locusts & primaries tell the time of year
but not what year it is; I forget and
it's another breakfast as I
think of you
a smallest thought but it scalds
like a splash of fresh birdblood, hot hot that
blisters wishes so their dead skin peels
and all my other thoughts are pinker, flushed,
their nerves at surface.
     Listen,
you who can't hear anyway,
anyone who thinks of you
speaks another language right away,
an English so edged accurate intricate
it is yours only, only your
own mother tongue.
And how you do go on: you say
words in your language
again in my head, yes that's your
resonance, the intimate
economy of your scorn for falseness
(you a terrible liar for that reason)
oh I can hear warnings
     warning me but I
remember anyway I curve
into the curve of your voice as if
into kind arms, savage again
& happy as when you held me holding you, I

forget why I left you, the *Times*
shakes a little in my hand, good mornings
shake a little in my throat, daylight
shakes in the sight you taught
of human beauty; it stirs in these faces
of live beings who have true speech,
whose hands have worked to wire them with words
recorded, until their flesh is all first love.

Someone once told me he thought that you
when last heard from talked like me.
I know I used to try to talk like you.
I don't know; maybe I still do.

GARDEN: PAEONIA
"SOUVENIR DE MAXIME CORNU"

The ground wants rain. Crouched here
I know it better than my own name
And doubt it less; if weeding I kneel low,
Very low, or lie flat, what difference—
It is a self-explained stance
For a person pulling weeds. Daughter
And mother, sustaining member,
A joke, a joker, an account,
Another Christ, a trespasser—
Crookedly, with passion, by chance,
The haphazard selves crisscross
As they drift making no distinction
Among the living the dead the lost.
On an ageless planet I plant
A city garden; I try to keep
Phone books numbered and alarm
Clocks punctual; friend, penitent,
Audience, am have been must
Soon and can never be; can't
Since aiming fatally to please
Grasp and am without rest
Absurdly none of these.

Out here all weathers. Indoors, none.
I juggle, jump-turn, jig, to face
As a paradox the clock-wise places
I also with dim despair perceive
As a continuum
                    in which everyone
How do we do it does believe.
The extempore dead could I suppose
Describe my location, if asked.
Deaf-mute we living, though we labor

At loving, are as if invisible one
To the other, despite much love.

I ask them, finally. "Mary and William.
Edward? Elizabeth. Joan."
And bend weeding the black ground
Around the plunged roots of a peony tree
Flowered with tongues of silken flame
Named for a woman on the horns of memory.
Peacefully present, the dead make no sound.

Of the most cherished among
The cherished living, I can see
Six playing croquet shaded by boughs
Of May-laden cherry and pear.
I pose no question there.
I claim no right to answers anywhere.
Pleasure lover, I love my worlds that rouse
So many pleasures, being mutable and fair.

Who am I? Who am I, that I should care?

Until in the midst of the green
Growing, this garden that I tend
With touching, out of a forgotten year
You sharp as love come clear.
Contraries flash into focus as
The promising morning draws to an end;
I am a woman, kneeling here.
I am a place in which you appear.
    Once we shared a city we have left.
    I think it back, that slum-jammed
    Dazzling citadel. Clocks crack,
    Admitting history. Stranger, sweet
    Acquaintance, you would rather be
    Disguised as a stopwatch or shotglass
    Or calm certificate of bonded dividends

But you speak, you say my name,
And say, "The ground wants rain.
It will rain soon"; I agree
And suffer fusion into something
Like simpleness, order, identity.

I recognize my hands.
By hands used to gardens
The heart fortunately thudding,
Continuous power continuous control
The body's beauty kept continuous,
Is felt for as is thunder,
Palms flat, pressed hard.

Soundlessly gentle, strands of rain
Stroke the stripped ground;
Rain follows rain, quickening.
Spread as they say eagles are,
Stretched as if like rain across air,
But on earth I have made green, familiar,
I arrogate to my embrace
The almost afternoon, praising
Such sequences as this unbreached
Spiral of weather; turning,
It turns: Pinnacled, crystal,
Spindled with prisms, lucent
Under arrowless opened skies,
The towers of air spin off
A glistening morning floss
To thread noon with shimmering.
Drawn
To the upper air the sea
Returns to the sea.
Haze mist downpour; splendid;
I'll be drenched. Gently
Drunk, I think, "In this world
This is the welcome due a citizen."

· · ·

Under the warm rain I am under
The warm rain makes run together
Earth, its seas and meadows;
Woman, child, crone;
To expect, to remember, to be;
All perfectly separate, all perfect
Known separately; now all seen through
                One color.
It becomes me where I lie
Gratefully, when I recognize
My glad ghost fixed with surprise
Having learned who cares and why
Color trembles from variety to light

Until as midday strikes I ask
If we are each other's accidents
Structured into the everyday air;
Until like a planet's rings around
A planet and its proper atmosphere
Your afternoon answer makes
A ring around me mapping my
Geography, "Your many and your one
Are to use as you please. My dear.
Like honey the morning sun
Has packed the honeycomb."

I hear and midground midday
Midway in an auspicious midyear
Come full tilt home;
I tell the time, take the glass
Incredulously; hope-
Ridden, I read and see
This birth certificate
Belongs to me.

It says I am of age and a native.
It says I am born free.

INFORMATION

1

Open early to the runes
Of children waking I pace out
The maze of table setting: honey, bread,
Hot milk, butter, loud forks & spoons,
Unmatched cups. The runes reduced & read,
The brilliant mix of voices disperses
As separate embodiments of worlds go out the door.
Expert, I rise, rinse, shelve, restore
Objects to interim order, then sit & pour
Tea from a glossy pot; lucid, as defined
By the cup, it is an oval, circumscribed;
It smells of the smoke of coastal
Hills soft as Southern Sung, gold-shadowing,
In the China of the mind
Only faintly trembling.

2

Rectilinear, the brittle window shapes
For me its landscape version of the world.
Down from a blown March sky rhythms of distance
Intersected by darts of bird
Ripple into a diagonal of rise
Of roof next door and a description
Against the light of oakfact & maplefact.
A cherrybranch tapping the glass
Acts as the groundplane. Dimensions interact
As the line of the wind races through
Composing it, making the composition live.
Mornings, as dozens of seasons have shifted a little
Becoming each other,
I face up to this.
It is informative.

3
I'm lucky; I'm unstruck, not starving; so
I think about what I'm seeing; I abstract
From the crammed nets of rod and cone the catch
My mind takes in for factoring

But when the network breaks with my wanting, sharp,
What is more than rational, to know,
Shorted, I eccentric flow
Sightless into what I see,
Out I go unhanded, feeling for ways of being:
My flecks of blood cool to build the limevein
        pale in the grey stone;
Axons push with the upthrust and downthrust of crabgrass
        climbing the molecular arch of the clawroot, the blade;
        dendrites flower fragile in the seedtassels;
My bones hold it, stressed in steel ceilings;
Borne along unsupported as cloudmist, I lost drift
Exorbitant.

A great recreation
It's nothing remarkable
A flying out a sparkshowering outering and
When searching out persons always one target
        right to the habitless leap of the heart
How contained the stone lies almost still in its changing
How frantic the heat in the sparrow's wingbrain, how subtly
        the close structure of feathers like flowerstalks
                plumes to be lofty
How at home you move marvelling
        where you live looking
        for nothing particular
How valuable the tip of your little-used
        left earlobe
How shy we are

GLIDING

A.M., TOWN GARDEN
Sometimes, riding the thermals, the swallows
drift backwards a little at their ease
before they tilt, slide forward down,
and drive their blades of wings stroke on stroke
to catch another column of wind; it lifts
them and they soar. It's a spinning soaring
in the morning windchange; tight
spirals take them to such heights they
vanish; viewed ecstatic, edge-on at their
curve into sheer sky, they turn as
invisible as the principles of flight
        all this time crying
        short crying
—the "i"s and "e"s of excellent action—
to say their only
effort is the effort of the act:
sounds we have all sometimes needed,
never made, and seldom deserved
to have a hearer hear.
I look up at them from shade in a walled
well of green among roses and boxwood.
To practice is to take a chance on joy, I think;
the one use of what they do is skill; skill
works against limits to cancel out
sloppiness, tedium, and some pain;
one skill is plenty; taken to the full
is morning swallow-soaring, easily
voicing the sounds of inner
rejoicing in its readiness.

P.M., MOUNTAIN FLIGHT TERRAIN
To look out from high places without flinching
(I do it belly to the ground) is to suspect how speech

might work, were we ready to face
the drop
into our inner space and find for mind
however awkwardly words and syntax
to negotiate aloud what otherwise
is mystery. It is to suspect our
gravity would change could we surface
the words of that integrating music
we all hear privately.

Hang-gliders haul their gear up here.
They've worked for years to manage a freedom.
They sleep under schema of da Vinci drawings,
keep calculators, wind-tables, equipment catalogues
in the bedside table drawer.
They have passion, brag, argue, share
their dozens of small implements of skill,
their geometry, costumes, support
facilities; train like acrobats,
measure up to standards; are licensed,
play. Clumsy, thick-boned,
beautiful, they practice doing
what they are not suited to;
a second of horror
collects their massy bags of flesh dense
with life and throws them out over
8,000 feet of moving air, as they aim to catch
with the fabric of their thought-up wings their
sustenance. They take flight: people
sail among eagles, as alert,
electric, spending as the mad.
They change the axioms, until
after short soaring,
they home in on a managed
flat of mowed green ground. Sometimes
they can walk back up whole mountains
to their cars, imagining
the next leap into longer independent flight.

. . .

Though they'd seem to need wings not hands
to endure the insubstantial field,
having made wings by hand,
they face it readily. It is so huge
it solicits the delight
of those who live open-armed; they
afford it; they enter its emptiness
in a posture of embrace.
Their point of view
would torment others, the hungry,
the cramped and landless, the sad,
who would look through the fields of joy at
the thousand horizontal miles of growing ground
whose juices might, in season,
alleviate their ancient needs.
I'm the ordinary middle of these extremes.

My skill is small and local;
like many ordinary people
I scan the closer mystery: thinking
we want the skill to press against
the limits of our speech, we rehearse
the accents of the inner world, tuneful but
invisible, in hopes the outer ear
will quicken to thought spoken
until
       across the empty air
of personal separateness—and all
are separate—we will sound true or
human to each other,
human kind,
hearing, heard, and
recognized. We elect
readiness to practice this.

Straight ahead of me is sky.
It is wholly flourishing. Below it & me

the earth in its rock-fold distances
is starred by geodes of inhabited villages
where cliff & gorge divert the winds.
Three hundred years ago they snaked a crazy
carriage road over this maritime Alp
just below these heights. Once a woman
kept an inn on it, and help for horses.

The air is ripe. My fists unclench,
and the air, filled with the odor of
thyme & lavender I lie on, fills my hands.
Unshaken by my readiness
or the smallness of my readiness
—or my ignorance of how
the hollows in our speech will fill
as we rehearse aloud against our limits
the names and principled tunes for shapes
and fragrances and absences of shapes
we have in mind—
I envision the next leap, the next
thousand years of practice,
the eventual skill
become like independent flight, habitual.

THE GREAT DEAD, WHY NOT, MAY KNOW

for Joan Paul, d. April 1978

No grief goes unrelieved;
some days, half meaning to,
I turn my undefended back
on the grey & snarling scene
of my dissociating pack
and hope.

Some suppose that this post-natal life
where all we have is time, is fetal life,
is where as we bounce and flex in time
our years of moons change us
into beings viable not here
but somewhere attentive. Suppose,
borne down on, we are birthed
into a universe where love's not crazy;
and that split out of time is
death into a medium where
love is the element we cry out to breathe,
big love, general as air here,
specific as breath.

I want to talk to those outlanders
whose perspective I admire;
I listen often to the voices of the dead, and
it feels like my turn in the conversation.
I want to ask, say, Yeats (or
someone else it would make sense to,
Crashaw, Blake, H.D. who
worked out Sappho's honey simile,
Joan word-lover you too, all you
who know what English has to do
with a possible answer)

· · ·

And I'd say, to set up the question:
Listen,
after over a hundred lifetimes
of summers of honey since Sappho's,
of beekeepers (who set out orchard
rows of nectarplants to bloom
before and after the appletrees,
  who sow alfalfa or tupelo,
  clover or roses,
  "all roses," all summer,
then break the combs out of their dark
and decant the honey heavy & flowery)
—listen, it's no different.
Honey's still dangerous.
Honey's pervasive.
Hunger for honey scalds if satisfied.
I know; I walk around dry-lipped;
my throat burns, and the August air at noon
ices it as I breathe because
I've been eating honey right from the spoon

and (as you, outside observers, can recall)
though petal & pollen nod golden & mild,
honey here burns like gall
and, having burned bitter
  sweet raw hot
generates a language for wild
love not limited to pollensoft
couplings of lovers; it generates
the longing to use that language
though there be not any one
to speak it to. Such honey
expressed as if it must be as love
which colors all encounters and lasts
long after one love has gone to seed,
changes the throat of a speaker
till it aches with expectancy
as it asks:

. . .

WHAT (as at last I ask
        you of the outland honeyed universe,
        you great dead)
what do you do with love
when it is no more sexual
        than I am sexual,
when it is general
—in me, not mine—
and yet shapes the air,
like breath, like a honeyed
breath of air carrying
meaning between
me and everything there is;
when as if it must it defies
my daily exercise of savagery
and cause for guilt;
when it is absolute,
too sudden to disguise,
unmapped,
unlocalized,
stubbornly addressed
to any eyes—
though it find me no less slothful nor
in any way more kind or wise?

What but
(since the love is in the language)
call it hope
—that helps a little—
and hope to imitate your inlands of example
by praising the possible;
what then but praise the ripening
cure of language which plays
among questions and answers
mediating even love and grief,
what but
        —as the window the morning

as the foot the tilt of the ground
as the river the lights of its city—
praise how the actions of language or honey
seem in their transport to express,
from the collected heat and sweetness
of hearing and speaking,
something
smaller and more human than belief,
some reason to read these thick omens
as good and those outlands as relief.

THE GREEN DARK (1988)

––––––––

to Rosemary & Leonard Deen

"sublime energizers"

ON A LIBRARY OF CONGRESS PHOTO OF EUNICE B. WINKLESS, 1904

Eunice, flexible flyer of summer, rides
across the noon fair
short-stirruped astride
her tall white mare,
her power implied
loosely in a practiced grip.
Her life is in her hands;
her living found, she lets nothing slip.

The pool glints like a tame star on the ground.
The ramp up the two-story tower, if
ramshackle, is ready.
Martial music starts.
Here she comes bareback. Having hitched
her triple-flounced Gibson-girl arts lightly
about her, her hands rein calm in.

Regal as Iphigenia
taking the upward course
in a drift of white eyelet muslin
she rides the animal horse.
Merrily fife & drum pace
their climb. Women think prayers,
set to not-look, just in case.
Men do not snigger, forget
their faces/ladies/bets, and stare
once she reaches the platform.
Music quits her exalted there.
Sounds, gathered to silence, swarm
stormhead about her stance. This crowd, knowing
horses, wonders if the big mare
shudders as it holds still. The pool shows
flatness: no wind. That's good. A brittle

drumroll rains. The drumsticks stop.
She leans to the mare's neck, smiling a little.

Out & groundless horse & girl drop
flying clear of equilibrium
Her body jockeying air
touches only bridle & with one
knee, horse, as nothing to spare
they head for the hope they head
in dread in dread for the pool.

To herself she says among her wet hair,
"Did it again. Damn fool."

I need her dreadful ease, its immense self-reference.
I watch to catch her hand-span skill address
the radius of her practice then guess,
self-tested, at its circumference.

Yet since I made all this up from one snapshot
it is fictive ink, not history.
What I think of her may be ready or not
to be telling. Who can make sense?

And, when do I act on better evidence?

The Story of the Problems

THE PROBLEM OF FREEDOM & COMMITMENT

In her first dot-to-dot book of puzzles
the last one left undone looks too hard.
It has hundreds of numbers. She prefers
the two-digit ones that trace out as
big-headed animals with big eyes
but she decides to give this one a try.
Soon she has a notion of one part of how
the picture will turn out to be.
She doesn't like it. Not one bit. She sees
it may be more trouble than it's worth so she goes
slower, hunting for the next consecutive
numbers, no longer anxious to find them
but anxious once they're found, fixed on,
and another strand of line goes down.
"It's too much. It's all mixed up," she thinks.
"Even the good parts are scribbly. There are
millions of books like this, all different;
I could just leave this mess and get
a new book, with no horrors in it,
a nice one, that I'd like." But she goes on
absent-minded, thinking *picture,* working out
the one she's started, worse and worse.
Right now there's nothing else to do, and if, she thinks,
she's false to this the first unpleasant one,
which is so complex her predictions are guesses,
which could be the most important one in the book,
maybe the puzzle will make her take a second look
and nothing she starts on will ever get done.

THE PROBLEM OF SOCIAL GROWTH

From an enthroned woman to whom she brings
her careful grab at dangle of brass ring
she accepts a nod as victory.
Large hand to small, a ticket has conveyed
that they are two graces whose smiles agree.
A winner, she blushes at accolade,
thinks she shd offer Crackerjacks
but can't. The ticket is green, torn short.
She finds the starter man and gives it back,
the token of power, her first earned passport
to a discus world a woman oversees.
She finds her best outside horse, climbs astride,
and spins Olympic on the victory's
round momentum that grown-ups, she thinks, ride.

THE PROBLEM OF THE EXPERIMENTAL METHOD

Today she learns that up is marvelous.
Water rises up unseen, falls, and appears
as crystals, their difference too sharp for us
to see without a magnifying glass,
or save, or savor. She feels ridiculous
(a scrap of velvet on her glove, a mass
of squashed snow underfoot) trying to dry
the lens, land a flake on velvet, and look.
It's not necessary. She feels like a spy.
She'd rather find snow pictures in her book
and read (and agree) about earth's atmosphere.
Cold. Experiments don't take her far.
Words do, without policing. Words keep here, here.
Their gravity homes her, on her native star.

THE PROBLEM OF FICTION

She always writes poems. This summer
she's starting a novel. It's in trouble already.
The characters are easy—a girl
and her friend who is a girl
and the boy down the block with his first car,
an older boy, sixteen, who sometimes
these warm evenings leaves his house to go dancing
in dressy clothes though it's still light out.
The girl has a brother who has lots of friends,
is good in math, and just plain good which
doesn't help the story. The story
should have rescues & escapes in it
which means who's the bad guy; he couldn't be
the brother or the grandpa or the father either,
or even the boy down the block with his first car.
People in novels have to need something,
she thinks, that it takes about
two hundred pages to get.
She can't imagine that. Nothing
she needs can be got; if it could
she'd go get it: the answer to nightmares;
a mother who'd be proud of her; doing things
a mother could be proud of; having hips
& knowing how to squeal at the beach laughing
when the boy down the block picked her up & carried her
& threw her in the water. If she'd laughed
squealing he might still take her swimming
& his mother wouldn't say she's crazy, she would
not have got her teeth into his shoulder till
well yes she bit him, and the marks
lasted & lasted, his mother said so,
but that couldn't be in a novel.

．　．　．

She'll never squeal laughing, she'd never
not bite him, she hates cute girls, she hates
boys who like them. Biting is embarrassing
and wrong & she has no intention of doing it again
but she would if he did if he dared,
and there's no story if there's no hope of change.

THE PROBLEM OF REVOLUTION

On a spring evening late in Lent
she turns 16. The saying she's hated,
"never been kissed," is correct nonetheless;
she likes best a boy she's never dated.

The rose of her dress is ashes of roses,
she's told; & its eloquent silk has quite
a good hand to it. Its self-belt shows, at last,
a waist—though flat not fashionably slight
& round. Her garter-belted stockings
are silk. The garter belt is net & blue.
The cake is strawberry pound, her favorite,
from Dean's. There are fresh strawberries too.
Facing the windows, with mirrors back of her
repeating outside green on the inside view
of presents wrapped & piled, she sits between
the scented aunt who thinks her new
and the cousin, ten, who sees her old.
As she blows out the counted certitude
she turns into still mirror water, cold
at the end of the family table, and comes untrue.

THE PROBLEM OF GRATIFIED DESIRE

If she puts honey in her tea
and praises prudence in the stirring up
she drinks, finally,
a drop of perfect sweetness
hot at the bottom of the cup.

There will be
pleasures more complex than it
(pleasure exchanged were infinite)
but none so cheap
more neat or definite.

THE PROBLEM OF LOVING-KINDNESS

She has gone soft
her body suddenly
lovely to her.
Gratefully
she wants to speak & be
believed, to see
his eyes darken with quiet & deepen
learning they agree.
But he believes as if deaf
what he says—
words for shocks of love that sound like
invincible grabs snatches whams hits, like
Cuchulain's *tae bolga*—a weapon that striking
her anywhere would shoot, in an electric
flex of tentacles, need of him
through every member, follicle
of hair, & finger-end—its thousand hooks pointed
so backward & sharp they must be endured
because to remove them would eviscerate.
She has to turn down his talk. She says
if love struck her like that she'd refuse.
If crazed endurance were the only ecstasy
she'd opt for evisceration on the spot.
She feels flat-footed, he's so carried away.
Since he's not listening she's silent;
she eats the rest of what she has to say,
her dreadful dowdy words,
the kind he won't hear,
full of dumb feeling,
"My darling. My dear."

THE PROBLEM OF OUTSIDE IN

Big trees make
the east field dark first. A shadowy
rabbit emerges. Shadowy grasses shake.

The archaic red-gold
that washes far slopes in one gold-red
rims tree-crowns in the west hill-fold.

From their leaves, under-lit
as the sun slips down,
their trunks dangle toward
the blur of ground.

Each such dusk, on the tallest tree top
a robin alights, silent, faces west,
& to the last warm flush presents
its heraldic breast.

She persists as she must, attendant on grace
to say this place into the place she meant,
till she perches as in all real places
on a cliff at the edge of a continent.

THE PROBLEM OF THE DARK

Lacking electric light
or other artifice
the instruction of night
is hit or miss.

Strolling's a dream-state
nightmare to run.
Fields she negotiates
drop to canyon.

She makes her foot wait, feel for
what's next. She's far in.
The edge of the work of her war
is air on skin.

THE PROBLEM OF THE FUTURE

She no longer expects gardens
will have low gates to Eden in them
or in a burst of roses,
flaunt truth from stem to stem

but, because of lovers (who must be
Eve or Adam to what they will see
as the last cement hardens)

the command grows:
to prophesy such gardens.

She prophesies such gardens.

WEARING THE GAZE OF AN ARCHAIC STATUE

The juggler in her suit of nerve
is eyes and hands. The rest of her
dangles soft-shoe below her shoulders,
relaxed, co-operating. She knows
that to toss things out is something
but not much, not important; is
for the sake of when, picturing
a ribboning like water spurting,
she is holding nothing.
She is on her own here;
she is not just letting go,
and her small touching skill is:
holding nothing.

Holding on, she is not a juggler.
She is you and me, hands full of things
she must practice juggling to get out from under.
She sets her feet and begins.
She smiles like Pomona, offering
three, a dozen, lifeless, bits & pieces she
can't get rid of; she presents them as
shapeliness and they lose weight.
The rhythm clarifies something, maybe her.
She settles back, a laughing fountain
pumping particles.
The order of motion emerges.
Up they loft one by one, she is tossing,
up, spheres, sticks, boxes, soft, metallic,
out with them she goes till her hands
close on nothing, are just
touched for the electric
seconds of netting the elements

with energy in air.
They drop, sprout, up, out, drop, up, & slowly
each touch makes her invisible save as
a phase of the great legislation
she proposes to obey.

"Love Is Not Love"

. . . love is not love
Which alters when it alteration findes,
Or bends with the remover to remove.

William Shakespeare, SONNET 116

"LOVE IS NOT LOVE"

for Elena Cornaro, first woman Ph.D., Padua, 1647;
and for those whose children are in pain here and now

It is cold. I am
drawing my life around me to get warm.
Holes in the blanket can't be rewoven.
Some thorns caught in it still scratch. Some tear.

I reach for comfort
to the left-out lives of women here and gone.
They lend them willingly. They know my need.
They do not hate me for crying. It beats despair.

Elena Cornaro
hands me her cinderella cap & gown.
I put them on. Stiff fur. But intact: she
(when eleven! just in time) saw

in a flash the mortal needles
their rain of cupidity
aimed at eyes across the looking air,

laughed and in singleness averted them
shielded by choice against the dark & steel.
She stopped herself in herself, refined
her will, and brought her mind virgin to bear

stretched across nine languages—nine sun-
keepers, their word-clusters grapes
of intellect, for wine
she pours me now.

It stings like speed:
Ph.D., TB, breath on fire, young,
she sported her doctoral vair
in vain. She too died of blood.

Yet the mind she trained
had warmed her in the storm
(all storms one storm) where
she'd left no hostage howling to be freed,
no captive mouths to feed;
in her sight, no punctual winter swarm
of guilt—pale bees whose attack breeds
paralysis, and dread of snow
that masks the snare.
I am stuck in cold. It is deaf. It is eiron.

What has happened to my child
is worse than I can tell you
and I'm ashamed to say
is more than I can bear.

Elena, listen.
My body speaks nine languages but the greed
of me is stuck, my exposed eyes prickle,
I think blank, he's lost out there, I'm scared.

What I have borne, I bear.

Oh I praise your continence, kind life, pure form.
Your way's one way, not mine; you're summer-stopped;
my meadow's mud, turned stone in this icy air.

Whose fault is it? It's at the root my fault.
But in your cape, I come to?
And I'm in your care?
As he is mine, so I am yours to bear
alive. He is still alive. He has not died of it.
Wronged. Wrong.

Regardless love is hard to bear.
It has no hospital.
It is its own fireplace.
All it takes is care.

. . .

Well, when you grew intimate with pain,
what did you do. How did you do it. Where.
That, this? Thanks. Suppose I'm not in time,
Is it worth a try. I'll try,

try to conceive of room to spare,
a surround of walls steady and steadying
an uncracked ceiling & a quiet floor,
a morning room, a still room
where we'd bring mind to bear upon
our consequences—we who make
no difference, who ignoring
absence of response have chosen
ways to love we can't go back on
and we won't,

regardless:
like your holy aura, Elena,
like your singleness, my fertility,
your tiny eminence, your early death;

like our Vassar Miller, her persistent listening;
like our Tillie Olsen, her persistent flowering;
like our Djuna and our Emily
their insolent beauty visored,
disguised as hermit crabs;
like our Sarah Jewett's faithful gaze—
cast down—
like my long-drawn-out mistakes.

Elena maybe we
remember each other as room
for when to cry, what to cry for,
cry to whom.

HANGZHOU, LAKE OF THE POETS

For Joe and Heather Cuomo

MORNING

Reading the bones, wetting a fingertip
to trace archaic characters, I feel
a breeze of silence flow up past my wrist,
icy. Can I speak here? The bones say I must.
As the first light strikes across the lake, magpies
scream, and the cast bones say the work must come true,
it's been true all along, we are what we do
out on our digs. Dictor and looker, all eyes,
with spade and a jeweler's loupe I sift mud & dust
for bone, for shellcast. Spy, archeologist
of freshness, I expect sight-made-sound to reveal
fear cold at the throat of change, and loosen its grip
so that mind, riding the bloodwarm stream, wells up
as the speech that bears it and is telling.

EVENING

Magpies scream. Though the tongues of birds
say Now and warn forward, free of a live past,
we seek back and forth for change, the ghostly sparkling
of our watertable under everywhere.
If I don't speak to tap & ease it out,
I go dry & dumb & will die wicked.
On the lake of the poets a stone lamp flickers.
It casts eight moons dancing, casting doubt
on the moon that rides above the winter air.
Ice thaws in a poet's throat; the springing
truth is fresh. It wakes taste. The taste lasts.
Language floods the mud; mind makes a cast of words;
it precipitates, mercurial, like T'ang discourse
riding the tidal constant of its source.

LEVELS

A stone fence holds the heat.
Close to it, the earth face opens:
a little eye
rimmed with dirt crumbs;
a nerve inside winks
alive with ants.
The yellow-shafted flicker
before it strikes inspects
the spot, drops
from the fence, calculates,
lifts the lid off.
Air fractures, and
inner alleys collapse, as
diamond-cutter the flicker
like a good writer starts
at the heart.
Its bill its tool,
it chisels toward the fault,
beaks at the crux of it, and
chambers of egg-cases
crack open. As the bird
eats, insects by hundreds
scatter in patterns carrying
clustered eggs, rushing
some to safety, later.

Ants leave me cold,
their bitty parts reflexive,
like cells of lung or muscle,
unprincipled, lacking
a visible body to serve—
oh, why qualify. Ant-mystery
drifts out of mind.

The bird is flicker;
its action exhibits it,
pinioned to a wheel which
the mind's eye axles,
the mind's eye spins.

THE ROYAL GATE

Little Jacqueline Pascal played with Blaise
reinventing Euclid (Papa told them to).
While he made up conic sections, she wrote plays
& got papa out of jail when Richelieu
liked her long impromptu poem in his praise.
I haven't read her verse. It's not in print.
Blaise invented: the wristwatch, a kind
of computer, fluid mechanics, the hint
for digital calques, probabilities,
the syringe, space as vacuum, the claims of lay
theologians. He thought (he thought) at his ease.

In her convent Jacqueline kept the rules.
On or under every desert there are pools.

OUTSIDE THE FERTILE CRESCENT

Too long out of her seashell, too far away
from green waves sparkling as they lick the sky,
Aphrodite falters. Shallow ponds delay
her sea-search. Off course, inland, tired, dry,
she takes a man's words seriously
when he offers water. He owns a well.
She settles in his oasis. His one tree,
his human heart, cast their spell;
for such implosion she serves him gratefully.
He keeps her safe from his city of those
who are wicked. She gets water enough,
cupfuls, pitcherfuls, to cook & wash clothes,
not to plunge in. Pillared when she calls his bluff,
at dawn her salt crystals gleam, flushed with rose.

DREAM OF TOO LATE

for Léon King

I come to tall, with a
shock in my banquet-hall,
two-dimensional this time.
As the crux of the decor I'm
honored, though woven flat & hung bold & high.
Every-colored, slightly rippling, I
supervise, magnificent, a tapestry
worthy, one of Nine Queens all praise readily.
My crown in gold thread forgives my face.
Too late I see how I earned this pride of place.

Too bad. I want to start over, to be
brief, a briefest agent of tranquility.
I'd be willing to be lily, to grow
set out in April in a tub below
the south casement where under stroke of sun,
lilium, I'd slowly, candidatum,
open my bells, one by shining one.
I would not mind how soon such work is done.
I'd be animal, bird, vegetable,
anything as useful as delible,
the opposite of icon. I wanted me
as easy to alter as air, subtly
tranquil
      like her, there, the younger
sister the harper
makes up a poem for, which he as is proper
does not sing until after his astute
praises of host and hostess. She causes no stir
as she ascends his wit.
                  She takes her lute
(a page brings it, gilt, small, three strings).
She pushes back her hair and sings,

and—though no one can hear her
since she is only the younger—
instantly everyone's cup is clean, bright, full
of a supreme wine,
its ripe light still.

PLOT SUMMARY

Time threads the random in the order of thought.
The basic survey course (*Gawain* to Milton;
Dryden to Yeats) spreads a net where, once caught,
Webster leads a reader strand by strand to Donne.
Memory weaves a long life's small events
to a tissue of intelligible days.
Some pique the whole length with a figured suspense;
some vanish. The whole plot whole cloth displays
gives time consequence (I met him, then her;
we read Joyce out loud; I had a black silk dress.)
The past persuades me to trust the calendar
and I do—unless I sleep or unless
some wind, some scent like the Hudson low-tide stink
splits time & I think *you,* and *you* are all I think.

SYNTHESIS

Elemental as weather this love
is of delicate appetite.

Leaves must reflect to the air
the surfeit of light they eat.

You are tender as lettuce;
your mineral bitterness is
suspended in sweet water,
my health in its element.

SPRING SONG

Many May nights I've longed, and failed, to see
the singular mating-flight of the woodcock, whistling
up like a moon-target arrow, warbling loud but voiceless,
song shedding fibrous from the instrumental self,
wings slip-streaming a firm sound as they soar.
With luck, I dream of the body of song I've read of
& sometimes sat up, well placed, waiting for.
November, & I wake moon-laved, too late
for the display a woodcock makes—so extreme
that for once in the work of species for their genes
once is enough. May is behind us, that light.
Here are two solid bodies, wingless, bodies of friends
who are never lovers, bare of former wife and
former husband and usual circumstance.
We are two bony poets horizontal under
the wash of moon, its ennobling shadows.
Both love the display of structure,
the service of skeleton; coherence,
our stock in trade, supports the fleshly molding
of years and acts recorded as musculature.
Our lesson is: that our words embody our purposes.
These are decent mattresses
& the space between them wide enough to hold
what we do not need as friends, what lies outside
the writ of our small parliament for good.
Free to dream we do not haunt each other.
What I say when I talk in my sleep
I trust you with, so you may guess that across
my inner sky (as yours, I'd say)
the vertical longing soars.
We leave each other safe. I leave to dream
wings and wing-arms, wristed, hauling
the dark form, its bones full of air, in a surge

in a tube of whistling in a triumph otherwise
silent in unguessable flight, almost
making out in translation
the words of the celebrant
and the syllable it celebrates.

We are too early for the May that elsewhere
lies ahead, locked in its promises,
its power to invent: self as instrument.

DE-FUSING THE USUAL CRIMINAL METAPHORS

Pity the idle who (though daily our lives
must make room for those who use clubs guns knives)
speak as if a penis were, when erect,
a tower of hard. The dear part we inspect
is always quick to shrink from violence;
hand-small, it fits any woman well.
Jocktalk of huge dongs grown trenchant as they swell
stands in, to hide the gathered evidence
of our true brute force; it is greed, not sex,
that we secrete & feed, till it infects
the whole life not the part with rape-like impotence.

The part comes on hopeful, nudging, nuzzling, tip
bent damp and rosy toward a soft eclipse.
Here's no jackhammer jammed home ruthlessly
but the yielding press of stamen under bee,
glowing at the sweetness of us; neatly met
and heedful (clumsy) as we sweat.
Here's no plow, ramrod, sword; no piercing cut—
if root, tender, a root-bud, just unshut;
though worm a word of yes and asking blessing,
though hole a blessing asking mouth of yes,
as one soft-tissued muscle noses plumply through
other muscles, their lax loop drawn. Here, we two
make touch our second sight as, no longer blind,
we each bring a self—big bones, guts, thoughts, hearts—
to local focus, trusting the ease we find
beyond discovery of our nervous secret parts
(as if hot trust might disinfect our minds
and its oils ease the human kind in us
to be in public as in private generous
with exchanges larger than the ease we're thinking of;
as if what we have to make in making love is love).

JAMAICA WILDLIFE CENTER, QUEENS, NEW YORK

On a south wind the sea air off
the flats and inlets of Jamaica Bay
mirrors as they do,
almost wavelessly, space recast as
flatness, long
diminishings of blue
borne lightly in toward
earth colors, steel-lit ochres,
rose-mucky brown, greens.

I am a window that takes this in
like a door, or mouth.
I spit nothing out.
I wait—like the egrets,
egrets spread on distant trees
like a wash of table-linen
for the sun to dry.

Were I a room I'd be stuffed
but what windows admit
I transfigure
to the bite-sized images
intelligence eats & eats
eagerly.

Splotches of white
contract, lift
into springing figures; bird.
One by one, one is a leader, up
off the green dark
they go into sun.
They are coming this way
to lunch in the shallows.

I too am good at hunger;
it never deserts me.
I admit as I am able
frank delight
in the deaths and decisions
of visible appetite.
Deep delight;
it is for—not of—myself,
it is for you
I write
of the storage and freshness
of keepers
of the life
of appetite.

THE IDES OF MAY

(for my children entering parenthood)

Every seventh second the wood thrush
speaks its loose curve until in ten minutes
the thicket it lives in is bounded
by the brand of its sound.

Every twenty-eight days the leisurely
moon diagrams the light way, east to west,
to describe mathematics and keep us unstuck
on our arched ground.

Every generation the child hurries out of child-
hood head bared to the face-making blaze
of bliss and distress, giving a stranger power to
enter, wound, astound.

BETWEEN

for my daughter

Composed in a shine of laughing, Monique brings in sacks
of groceries, unloads them, straightens, and stretches her back.

The child was a girl, the girl is a woman; the shift
is subtle and absolute, worn like a gift.

The woman, once girl once child, now is deft in her ease,
is door to the forum, is cutter of keys.

In space that her torque and lift have prefigured and set free
between her mother and her child the woman stands
having emptied her hands.

HARD-SHELL CLAMS

When it was too late for him to provide
his own share in my happy childhood, my
father stopped clowning out stories & tried
for a whole day to see me—a good try
by both of us. Back we went to the seaside
of old summers, we two, we talked, we swam,
sleek with cocoa butter that caught the sand—
a glitter like chain mail guarding who I am
from his used blue gaze that stared to understand.
Closed, stuck closed, I watched us—far me far him—
go small, smaller, further, father, joy dim
in beach light. Our last chance, last perfect day.

We laughed. We ate four dozen hard-shell clams.
We swallowed what I would not let us say.

OUT OF EDEN

Under the May rain over the dug grave
my mother is given canticles and I who believe
in everything watch flowers stiffen to new bloom.

Behind us the rented car fabricates a cave.
My mother nods: Is he? He is. But, is? Nods.
Angels shoo witches from this American tomb.

The nod teaches me. It is something I can save.
He left days ago. We, so that we too may leave,
install his old belongings in a bizarre new room.
I want to kneel indignantly anywhere and rave.

    Well, God help us, now my father's will is God's.
    At games and naming he beat Adam. He loved his Eve.
    I knew him and his wicked tongue. What he had, he gave.

I do not know where to go to do it, but I grieve.

PATIENT

The woman sleeps, old hand under old cheek,
skin like white iris crumpled, baby-sweet.
She'd let herself go but she's too weak
to organize admission of defeat.
Morning. Her girl tries to get her to speak
but she's too busy with plans to protect
the one thing she doesn't dare lose, her own,
her married name, "i," not "e," that's correct,
not her first name, her whole name, hers alone
(first names can be anybody's). Some days
she can't say it so she writes it. They
steal her name. Eyes shut, she stares at warm haze.
Then she smiles as she remembers to pray:
Trust. Someone to talk to. Something to say.

MUSEUM OUT OF MIND

Whatever it was I used to call you out loud
when I was twenty, ten, or less, I forget. Odd—
I shy from recalling the syllables of how

the golden age once spoke (say, as we talked non-stop
after school, or having our hair done, or as you
chose green peas pod by pod while I watched you shop).

Later, myself mother, I called you the motherdear
no child of mine would use—but one of the baby
humwords must have come first. And I am infant here

before your advanced degrees in death, seeking speech
in words of a tongue I am spelling out of you who could,
by the stars and letters of a map you'd make, teach

(Queens Hermes, alphabet giver) anyone to find
the essential simple, and to translate all
locations into constellations of the mind.

I talk to your absence. Daft. Grotesque. I begin
to see you as grotesque, yes a joke, a guess,
a grotesque of the grave I wept to leave you in.

Birds love dead trees. They like to strip a shred of bark,
tug at it, shake it, lunch on egg-case and insect,
and I go after you like that. Graves are

grounded in the mind though the cemetery keeps
grounds & groundplan, their care perpetual; yours is
in the sad best section, comical—we Stoics

. . .

are all comics—among Mafia and their daily,
like you, communicant women. A solitary,
motherdear, you loved the look of community

as, dogged in practice, you believed undaunted
and behaved, relentlessly, as you believed,
so that at times your present company haunts me

like a storm of comic joy. Into the eight-body
plot grandma bought and put grandpa at the bottom,
she went next old raceme dry tiger lily;

then her son and then your man; there you now lie
kept from your father and mother by a layer
of brother and lover and also by

the costumes, wood bronze lead satin silk & wool,
you each wear. Now you, famous for the Saturday
museum-hauls of your New York, ignore the full

shelves of the Costume Museum Out of Mind
you have entered. Once your heels & skirtshapes looked to
Paris; now you notice none of the well-defined

custom samples, filed as fashion and history;
beaded dresses, bow ties, hard collars, French chalk,
corsets, false cuffs, union suits, hand embroideries,

and decades of dressed hair, an outgrown show of styles,
some rotted, some stained; yet in your choice place are stored
shapes & modes that amply record our tribal

grasp of the honor of family, the dignity
of ritual, the self of death. There is not much
nourishment in this but I beak it out. Better be

. . .

choking down images of the set greywebbed hair
cocoon your skull is wearing and the tumbled nest
of cowlick at your nape, than to grimace and bear

as I bear the packet I found in your drawer, kept
hidden for sixty years but kept: the lissome, fresh,
bright chestnut yard of hair you cut

to enter the nineteen-twenties. Dismay, dismay,
disgusting, it's beautiful, funny, it's yours, mama,
still in tissue paper, boxed, as I throw it away.

CALL

Child like a candelabra at the head
of my bed, wake in me & watch me as
I sleep; maintain your childlife undistracted
where, at the borders of its light, it has
such dulcet limits it becomes the dark.
Maintain against my hungry selfishness
your simple gaze where fear has left no mark.

Today my dead mother to my distress
said on the dreamphone, "Marie, I'll come read
to you," hung up, & in her usual dress
came & stood here. Cold—though I know I need
her true message—I faced her with tenderness
& said, "This isn't right," & she agreed.

Child, watched by your deeper sleep, I may yet say yes.

FRIDAY MARKET

(from Vence, for Mary Denver Candee, 1867–1940)

Under the arch, its ruined walls reused
as the house-stone of small piles of rooms
(one window each & that spilling flowers)
we enter Old City shadow
on weekly market day.
Tourists, we gossip,
amble, and inspect; handmade candles, sox;
a table strewn with herbs tied in bundles
by grasses, where a child learns her numbers
as her mother makes change; down the street,
leaf-wrapped goat-cheese local as radishes; and
a rosy person selling confections.
I want some. "I make them myself, at my house,"
she says, "of good ingredients."
We buy finger-long beige biscuits, fragrant,
seeded, very tasty, a sackful.
I feel cheerful and grateful.
I eat more than my share.

Days later I wake thinking, "Caraway"——seeds
of such kind sleep as we eat for the sake of descent
to the gone, where I look up safe, years ago.
Mother's mother smiles, shows me a plate of fragrant
caraway cakes, and says, "Take all you want."
I stop crying and do. The seed-bite is telling.
"We have plenty," she says, and I learn
that what she says is true.

MYOPIA MAKES ALL LIGHT SOURCES RADIANT

On the treed slope opposite, vertical
in a close weave of leaves, a giant
woman's face is visible, if
I focus into its shadow-spoken eyes.
. . . it is my face the one
I used to have when in that beauty
all the young own. Its look
is of unripe readiness.

When I put back on my spectacles
it is smiling thoroughly and
is ragged, wrinkled, very old,
its laugh-lines definite,
its softest estimates still
ready to unfold.
It is not symmetrical; one eyebrow
lifts; broad across the forehead
a lock of dark, hair or evergreen,
casts waving shadows.
About the mouth
there is something stricken,
some holm-oak silence facing north.
Winter is coming, giant double-face, old friend.
Winter will replace the persimmon
flagrant at your throat
and the lucky gold fig-tree crown.
To your evergreen mouth only the shape
of your evergreen brow will be
company, as the foliage goes down
flying, worn to the dry fibre,
making its light escape.

EN TRAIN

"Paris in 20 minutes." The old excitement
arrives on time as suburbs flash by,
ugly only to look at, lit, densely well meant.

Non-human nature behind us in the dark, I am shy
with longing. We switch to the rings of human intent.
I prepare myself with caution like a quick reply.

City twin to my scarred city on my continent,
Paris gleams, catacombed with greed. Its stained sky
rosy as with deity at midnight is my light tent.

Live sounds, ground small, pulse from it to electrify
roads that join cities into circuits of consent.
Geography is personal, a map whereby

every journey maps home ground. Confident
we're earth-borne, we can't get lost. I enter the event.

IN ABEYANCE

The day of the transit of raptors
happens every September along
the Hudson airlane or updraft;
bird-watchers set a month's mind for it.
No joiner, I'd never joined them
but today from dawn to twelve
high on Hook Mountain I took among friends
with windbreakers cameras binoculars
a watch at a station between fake owls
hoisted on posts facing north & west
to lure the sharp-shins in.
We had the luck to watch
over a hundred (a Cooper's, two marsh, a kettle
of fifty beyond the Tappan Zee); we spent
hours of disembodiment, selves tossed out to vision,
angels in our abeyance, taking gift as title. Tired,
I cased the glasses, ate apples & sandwiches,
lay supine on warm noon rock out of the wind
to magnify sleep with praises of lenses

and woke gasping at shouting, It can't be! It was,
was fluency, inverse above us for hours,
a river swimming with flying a mile deep
among the invisible: all otherness:
        affluence: as twelve thousand
hawks went over, broad-winged
(an eagle among them, osprey also)
the one species mostly; I saw them,
their undulance communal, some
dropping awhile a quarter-mile afloat
then pulsing up again deep.
            Hawks
splash difference on the visible the

virtual the not-so sky,
displaying the shaping of air
as they plunge up, into out-of-touch, or
as aloft they liquidly
maintain their openness
fully extended to a rest
that rides deeper in the cells
than sleep or than most desire gratified.
There they take their distance
and a stillness to see it in
that I will die knowing nothing inward of.

They know one thing: when.
Days dangle for them, dipping
down & up, then dip less & less
& slow, till left sun & right storm
halt at a balance, & ten thousand
high nests empty as all leap
forward southward from & to
the when of equilibrium.

Together they ebb from us, emigrant,
their perspective on or in
the now of air, transfiguring.

INSIDE OUT

Dawning on me calmly,
suffused with old rose, while
past the full, just, the cool moon
sinks through dolphin-grey
clouds going beige into morning,
into much more sun,

restlessness
begins to lift the mists
I have in mind, winds
variable, gusts of change.

Alert & quickening, like olive leaves
flickering, grey side, green side,
                    like a school of minnows
darting in shallows over their shadows,
                    like blackbirds at sunrise
their particles of whistles sped sliding
over local surfaces outward to space,

I walk into harvest looking
for its true seeds its flesh-concealed
answers and prophecies—
autumn in a climate so far
mild; migration weather.

PRESENT

Even out of doors there are doors to open.
The deep wild-scape, while they are shut, remains
as urban as TV and two-dimensional
as maps of space- or underwater-traffic lanes.

Portal to my tame attention,
wild beings gleam. A strangeness,
death-racing, gorgeous, goes
about their unknown business.

> The butterfly, fecund, its thousand of
> flown miles aimed for where there is milkweed,
> lights down; it closes its black-netted goldleaf
> camouflage over; opens; closes. Opens.

> The hawk makes its passes. Over the clearing
> its shadow slides, to the terror
> of mole & rockdove; jays scream blue warning.
> It abandons its soundless flight,
> drops, strikes.

> Just the sound of wings—crow clattering,
> fan-zip of chickadees, the hushed drift
> of owlfall—strikes, startles.

> Under oak, arbutus that
> gives its scent keeps its secret.
> Though it announce nothing, the shimmer
> at its edges warns: sweet life.
> > Found and in hand,
> the tree toad is all one pulse.

Though I learn about attention
and the sift of its waiting,

what trapped moments most show are further
doors shut beyond snatches, glimpses;
yet such presence ushers me, to where
though chances of being called do not increase
there is more chance of being present for the choice,
in the rush of Here I am that awe unlooses
with the gasp at unguessed difference.

ANALEMMATIC

Shadows matter.
Here in the country of the sun
the shadow of my body measures time.

"Bonnet De Villario struxit."
On a level in Vienne-on-Rhône
his gnomon takes his time.

I as hour-hand and observer of it
put my light-lack on a line
across the stone wheel-track of time.

Outside the squad of the Zodiac, feet joined,
I point my handshape at the spin
of rounders skipping to celestial time

and observe, I am engaged in day-praise:

> Accept, Interrupted Light, this short dark of mine
> personal and visible on account of time.

Take Time, Take Place

TAKE TIME, TAKE PLACE

I

There lay Lyonesse, a land now drowned.
There Iseut & Tristan acted, addicted
to love as catapult & drug of destiny.
There, beside themselves, they inflected
the story that shapes us, love misshapen
as fate, its gaunt greed beautiful.
Castle cave & philtre worn to sand & less,
legend washes up in the waters I drink
when, tired of walking free,
I long to abdicate to Lyonesse
in drunken fantasy:

     Our clean hotel room is sun warmed. As you
     close with me we sink & sink till we
     rise under each other borne over
     in the lifting falling lift
     of a slow tide quickening.
     We plunge where joy is, on a leash of air,
     and re-surface in a double
     ruffle of water; our joy crests
     as gasping shaky we draw separate breaths.
     Sea-water fills our cells
     while our doubling selves
     are kept apart by soul & skin.

As we dress we glimpse from the windows
the low-tide sea snarl, sunstruck above
where we may never walk among
the shadowshapes of fatal urgency,

for it is sunken, sunken,
that honeysuckle land,
its fort rings skyless, nothing left

but seven stones standing and they
under water at high tide.
It is lost, the desirable paradise
    where love greedy as dreams is fatal & excused,
lost, and the road to it
lost, and its amorous acts
pickled in brine.

Sleep take it. Awake I like a drier wine.

Though under the wish to sluice off
wounds and the memory of wounds
I dream I dive hand in hand
with both Iseuts, wordlessly
learning to live breathless their doomed way,
in fact even in that dark I feel a stricter lift
of longing for times of choice in the light of day

where I'd say many things to you but never
    lie and say, "I couldn't help myself";

where I'd have good dreams clear of doom & mystery
    and learn in from out, responsible as ecstasy;
where I might take time, take place, mind memory.

2
Time & travel change my mind.
Their implicit courses
make choosing more complex;
I lose the single scope
small choice protects.
All choices are losses—except
for true remembrance which sharpens
blunt intentions into acts,
or for false fantasy
which makes bandages of torn-up facts
to stem the haemorrhage of memory.

                    . . .

The landscape I have left behind
waits for me.
In fantasy, I need not remember it:
If I want, it is weather-free,
its mental climate generous;
I can call in, recklessly,
two moons or suns, calm or storm,
and any company.
Those I'd invite wd come peaceably,
the strong, the witty, but done with dispute—
Launcelot, Elizabeth, Finn,
Dilly Dedalus no longer mute
wd join my old friends, first love, lost kin
all looking as I'd wish they'd be,
at ease as hero & heroine.

Effortlessly helpful
like a southern slope, the people
at timeless picnics can praise a sky
clear without their hope;
they can agree about the food, real cream,
trees of sunwarm fruit, good bread.
They are the people I need
as much as solitude;
they'd all smile, according to this scheme,
not disliking me, not dead,
lost, or dischronous, but well met
and interviewed.

These haunts of wish are falsely true.

Real dream-work builds a windbreak
for retrieval & repair.
But I abuse it when I sleep awake,
to hide from grief I will not bear,
in its shadow-acclimated air.
It is rich, such nowhere.

3

Fantasies dampen the pang of cherishing
goods and chances lost or left behind.
I do no work; they can bring back everything
in waves of picture-music, filmy, soft-spined:
melons can bulge above thin greens of spring
as snowmelt swamps the brookbank to scare
big August moths while yes the applerind
reddens in flowering orchards, near where
live & dead share breakfast and at last find
intimate approval easy, in air
which such reverie, obliterating
absence, swindles to vision I can bear
since nothing is asked of me. Daydreaming
reforms loss till it is neither here nor there.

Loss reformed till it is neither here nor there
is double loss. Then let the absent shout
and shake pain's shameful scent on the air—
that will shock the old fact-faces out:
dank spring panic, my fate-embracing stare,
your rage, mine. Let the early dead speak again,
this time to untell the lies death left in doubt;
let their harsh loss start my resurrection
in the plural truth they were and are about.
Though the dead have sealed their eyes and arguments
and seasons irk or please us unaware,
marked in the far hawk and the daily wren
the great co-ordinates, perfectly fair,
might haul this place now up through that place then.

This place now—if hauled through that place then
whose salt inner seas lighten my real weight—
beaches my self in my shape, dries my skin,
& grounds me where I can stand to integrate
the crazy hot-cold climates I have chosen
or been chosen by. Bodies met in dream
that I once by drift-fire took to my embrace

confront me as stroke for stroke I redeem
that flesh with this. Time interpenetrates
the memory: match-flare, full blaze, fading gleam,
morning ash. Waking I see as they were then
the lost, towering, remote, but true, their beam
sentinel. I hear old names true-spoken
in the chuckle of the channeled inner stream.

Down the chuckle of the channeled inner stream
I stare for signs, imagining replies,
& endure in echo the spent grunts & screams,
the true relics of my victims & allies.
I squat & study what they meant to mean
and fail but listen: I've stopped saying yes
to the doom of being what I must despise;
doom is not self but a game, a guess,
a child's costume—and a deadly disguise
I can just get rid of like an ugly dress.
The hard sun of memory, in wisps of steam,
lifts off the make-up, the splotches of distress,
dries up the marsh-wraith veil of false esteem,
and sets off alarm-clocks sharp as happiness.

They set me off, alarmed at happiness,
to join birds in their sanctuary. A tern flies
tilting to its turns with acute finesse.
I watch it mediate marsh & beach, skies
and ocean, balancing stress & stress,
airlift & gravity, with unminded ease.
Its caught fish flashes, swallowed on the rise.
Its high speed fueled by its discoveries,
it pipe-threads upward as its black beak dries.
Its life embraces its necessities;
this federal parkland is its wilderness.
Such grace. It names the saving world I might seize
but am too locked in time to see: unless
we are what our imagination frees.

. . .

To become what my imagination frees
my road turns linear. Summer gardens die
awhile, above the ground's certain mysteries;
winter shines & deepens like a sleep; but I
leave Eden joyfully; all cyclic repose
dims the human joy I can't afford to lose,
the causeless joy that hears joy as a reply,
and turns my hand to what's left of my true
experiment in the forward of surprise.
Joy's like luck, imagine that! I can't
lose or win it, mean or wild, off or on my knees.
Joy speaks out. And in. The time-line joy may use
is broken and brightens not as I please
but any instant. Its innocence accrues.

On the instant, its innocence accrues
across the cityscape, real and immense.
Here bird and I are each other's news
alighting centered in the present tense.
Inside out I identify bird clues
framed in sun by my binocular guess;
here its lift of head & tail are evidence
its flash of song confirms; here is steadfastness
in single names for thick experience.
"Wren," I say. "Hawk." "Tern." "Luck." "Love." Wingless
and winged we startle then settle, each a view,
alert & modest in our different dress.
I hear unearned joy pay my human dues
and take this passage for my new address.

Climbing the steps, awake, I wake to sense
how dream-tides shape all shores, their forward press
rich in suspended dissolute continents;
and deep under the seas' collapsing caress
are the porches and bridals of Lyonesse.

THE BIRD CATCHER (1998)

———

TO THE MUSE OF DOORWAYS EDGES VERGES

Tall in the doorway stands
the gentle visitor.
I catch my breath

    (She's quite deaf,
    not interested in
    details of my decor.
    Her few words amaze me.
    Her visits are irregular,
    brief. When our eyes meet,
    how I am drawn to her.
    I keep honey cakes, in case,
    in the freezer. Once
    she stayed for tea.)

She smiles. She speaks up, some.
Each word ravishes,
bright with the sciences
she practices
in the music business.

"One day, when you're not dumb,
you must come
to my place," she says,
and vanishes.

I

For My Old Self

"I'VE BEEN AROUND: IT GETS ME NOWHERE"

Cuncta fui; conducit nihil.

—V. AURELIUS

I am the woman always too young to be
holding the diamond the baby exulting.

I am the worker afraid of the rules & the boss; my
salary heats the house where I feed many children.

I am packing my bags for coming & going
& going much further than ever before.

> Though elsewhere gets me nowhere
> place is not a problem.
> Feet keep me going,
> the impressive exporters
> of what place is about. Maps—
> gold on parchment or printed
> Mobil travel ads—lay it all out.
>
> But over every place, time goes
> remote, a cloud-cover question.
> You, in love with your castle, your jet,
> your well-invested dollars
> and I with my moving
> dictionaries & binoculars
> are both almost out of it,
> too far gone to find a bin
> with stores of more time in.
> A decade, a week, a second, then
> time shrugs and shudders out of touch
> into a perfect fit,
> and that's it.

I am the dog I let out in the morning
wagging & panting at the open door.

. . .

I am the foresworn child in the swing
arching & pumping, practicing, "More, more!"

I'm the crossword puzzle time & place
bound at the end by their loose embrace.

RESTORING MY HOUSE

Her husband dead, my grandmother destroyed
every photo of herself. I helped find them,
did as she asked, and didn't tell.
"Paper ghosts," she said, "that's all they are."

Now I undo my packages long in storage.
Crowded in notebooks or folders,
stapled or separated anyhow,
scrawled or machine-stricken,
these are words someone had, some I
had to say, green or seasoned, for myself.

My hands feel dull. Paper-coating
nasties the pores shut. Dusty in windowlight,
some edges still cut mean. Crumpled, some chip.

I rise from the mess on the living-room floor,
yank the stuck flue open, match the first lot
to their fire-life
transparent in its speech.
It murmurs over them. Lullaby
of the unknown life-giver, faceless,
earlier even than Hertha,
the hearth's the oldest deity
and my good riddance.

Longing to clear out
the debris of keeping, I feed in
records of years I need no record of.
They have gone dry at last.

They catch and blaze. I hook out
the backlog, oak seasoned for welcome.

Already a little charred,
it begins to burn.

Nodes of sunspurt interrupt then spread the fire.
Its burning gestures are harmonious.
At each downfall compensation flares
in a quick tree of flame.

The leaves I have torn up
turn into the hum of a
budding comfort disclosing
along a tree of transforming.

This task is in praise of ancestors,
those still working fireplaces
to whom I come when the next task

is to get out from under, hungry
to open up images
into the presence of absence
of images, and change.

"TROIS PETITS TOURS ET PUIS . . ."

She gives him paper and a fine-nibbed pen;
he discovers the world and makes a map.
She gives him boots and a Havahart trap,
Peterson guides, tent, backpack, fishhooks, then
rehearses the uses of the North Star.

He leaves a trail of breadcrumbs down the road.
He mails back snapshots of himself & his load
borne almost a mile till he thumbed a car
& hitched to where he spread his picnic out.
His assets (food & use of gear) he lends
to the driver. He learns he likes to play fair.
That all this must please her he does not doubt.

His map omits her. His snapshots go to friends.
A fresh music fills her house, a fresh air.

OLD MAMA SATURDAY

("Saturday's child must work for a living")

"I'm moving from Grief Street.
Taxes are high here
though the mortgage's cheap.

The house is well built.
With stuff to protect, that
mattered to me,
the security.

These things that I mind,
you know, aren't mine.
I mind minding them.
They weigh on my mind.

I don't mind them well.
I haven't got the knack
of kindly minding.
I say Take them back
but you never do.

When I throw them out
it may frighten you
and maybe me too.

       Maybe
it will empty me
too emptily

and keep me here
asleep, at sea
under the guilt quilt,
under the you tree."

NORTHAMPTON STYLE

Evening falls. Someone's playing a dulcimer
Northampton-style, on the porch out back.
Its voice touches and parts the air of summer,

as if it swam to time us down a river
where we dive and leave a single track
as evening falls. Someone's playing a dulcimer

that lets us wash our mix of dreams together.
Delicate, tacit, we engage in our act;
its voice touches and parts the air of summer.

When we disentangle you are not with her
I am not with him. Redress calls for tact.
Evening falls. Someone's playing a dulcimer

still. A small breeze rises and the leaves stir
as uneasy as we, while the woods go black;
its voice touches and parts the air of summer

and lets darkness enter us; our strings go slack
though the player keeps up his plangent attack.
Evening falls. Someone's playing a dulcimer;
its voice touches and parts the air of summer.

INCOMPARABLE ASSUMPTIONS

The lilium (rubrum, tall,
leaves spiralled up its spike)
spreads like Siva elegant arms,
many of them.

To perform its counterbalancing
each arm is weighted at the end
with long buds, daily
thicker heavier.

Stemmed above them, terminal,
one bud's flying open, fragrant.
Its back-bending petals blush,
full of grace, for today.
(Today's the awkward August
Feast, August Assumption;
rubrum blooms late for a lily.)

For two months leaf-hoppers beetles
slugs have tried it but no luck.
Out from its stake it lurches
into direct sun to suck up more
("More!") light, shading the dahlias.
It does well here
free though staked firm,
delivered from evil by
the nature of rubrum, unable
to go wrong or to do right or
guess at good or evil done to it—
an innocence only natural.

It gives the gardener
unremarked behind such blossoming

a measure:
                    of the action & flavor
innocence would assume for her
(a habit of vigorous growth
throughout her!) if she
were vegetal and innocent.

THE TITLE'S LAST

Here's the best joke, though its flavor is salt:
the bad company I've kept, the bad risks I've run
have left me standing (a figure of fun
but) one at whose shadow some strangers halt.

I've been pole when some asked, so they could vault
supported, high as they like, letting me drop
intact, and roll safe to a grassy stop.
We've gone our ways with pleasure and without fault,
they to the next race, I to the next use
poles are put to by the great competitors.

Self-schooled I've been fish, ocean floors
wrinkling my shadow, flashing free, loose,
in my long survival of all I've done—
for sharks that bite me eat death by poison,
le requin qui me mord s'empoisonne.

GRADUAL

(on September 14, Feast of the Exaltation)

This serene and mortal afternoon
slides the late summer
down a course of outwardness.
I take it in.

Now & then soft gusts stir the air.
Between them sun fills the stillness, windless.
White pinetrees filter the sun rays.
Their needles glisten; the light's increased.

Jays on lookout shriek: Enemies!
Watch your back! The non-human cries
pluck me out of the hush I hide grief in.
Pain I've kept hoarded flares up & off.
It gets smaller. It goes on out
to roost with the jays, simmering down
under treecrowns invisible from here.

Slowly westering, full
light slips invisibly
toward slant.

Collected clouds thin out flat,
their gradual ribboning
just visibly eastering.

ONE IS ONE

Heart, you bully, you punk, I'm wrecked, I'm shocked
stiff. You? you still try to rule the world—though
I've got you: identified, starving, locked
in a cage you will not leave alive, no
matter how you hate it, pound its walls,
& thrill its corridors with messages.

Brute. Spy. I trusted you. Now you reel & brawl
in your cell but I'm deaf to your rages,
your greed to go solo, your eloquent
threats of worse things you (knowing me) could do.
You scare me, bragging you're a double agent

since jailers are prisoners' prisoners too.
Think! Reform! Make us one. Join the rest of us,
and joy may come, and make its test of us.

POURRITURE NOBLE

a moral tale, for Sauternes, the fungus cenaria, *and the wild old*

Never prophesy.
You can't. So don't try.
Lust, pride, and lethargy
may cause us misery
or bliss.
The meanest mistake
has a point to make.
Hear this—
what his vintner d'Eyquem said
once the lord d'Eyquem was dead:
    "The wine that year promised bad or none.
    He'd let it go too late.
    Rot had crawled through all the vines,
    greasy scum on every cluster
    dangling at the crotches of the leaves.
    Should have been long picked
    but he'd said, 'No. Wait for me,'
    off to wait on a new woman,
    grapes on the verge of ripe
    when he left. Coupling kept him
    till rot wrapped the grapes like lace
    & by the time she'd kicked him out
    the sun had got them, they hung
    shriveled in the blast.

    Well, he rode home cocky
    & bullied the grapes into the vats
    rot & all, spoiled grapes, too old,
    too soon squeezed dry.
                The wine makes.
    The wine makes thick, gold-colored,
    & pours like honey.
    We try it. Fantastic!

not like honey, punchy,
you've never drunk anything like it—
refreshing, in a rush
over a heat that slows your throat—
wanting to keep that flavor
stuck to the edge of your tongue
where your taste is, keep it
like the best bouquet you can remember
of sundown summer & someone coming
to you smiling. The taste has odor
like a new country, so fine
at first you can't take it in
it's so strange. It's beautiful
& believe me you love to go slow."

moral:

Age is not
all dry rot.
It's never too late.
Sweet is your real estate.

FOR MY OLD SELF, AT NOTRE DAME
fluctuat nec mergitur

The dark madonna cut from a knot of wood
has robes whose folds make waves against the grain
and a touching face—noble in side view,
impish or childish seen head-on from above.
The wood has the rich stain of tannin, raised
to all-color luster by the steep of time.

The mouths of her shadows are pursed by time
to suck sun-lit memories from the wood.
Freezing damp and candle-smut have raised
her eyebrows into wings flung up by the grain,
caught in the light of bulbs plugged high above.
She stands alert, as if hailed, with beasts in view.

Outside on the jeweled river-ship, I view
a girl's back, walking off. Oh. Just in time
I shut up. She'd never hear me shout above
the tour-guides and ski-skate kids. How I would
have liked to see her face again, the grain
of beauty on her forehead, her chin raised

startled; her Who are you? wild, a question raised
by seeing me, an old woman, in plain view.
Time is a tree in me; in her it's a grain
ready to plant. I go back in, taking my time
leafy among stone trunks that soar in stone woods
where incense drifts, misty, lit pink from above.

She's headed for her hotel room then above
Cluny's garden. She'll sit there then, feet raised,
notebook on her knees, to write. Maybe she would
have heard, turned, known us both in a larger view
and caught my age in the freshness of its time.
She dreads clocks, she says. Such dry rot warps the grain.

They still say mass here. Wine and wheat-grain
digest to flesh in words that float above
six kneeling women, a man dressed outside time,
and the dark madonna, her baby raised
dangerously high to pull in our view.
Magic dame, cut knot, your ancient wood

would reach back to teach her if it could. Spring rain.
Through it I call to thank her, loud above
the joy she raised me for, this softfall. Sweet time.

II

Separate, in the Swim

THE BORDER
(Annuals & Perennials, Mixed)

She kneels to the yellow short flowers
velvety, feathery, lit. Pansies
are for thoughts, she knows,
and, Pick lots but pick them
in the morning so they last.

The can of salted water is for slugs.
It kills them dead, quietly.
She finds one bigger than her thumb.
She looks away to drop it in but
hears it drop. She's taller this year;
standing she can gaze downward into
the iris Queen Maud a white crown
on the stem that presents it
above the crowded pansy border.

Next Saturday at Dorothea's wedding
she'll be the flower girl
with a crown of baby's breath clipped
to her slippery dutch-bob hair.

She must remember / she'd better practice
Left Foot First, this week,
every time she walks.
Grandma says, It's all right, dear,
all eyes will be on the bride.

The earliest tree peony is out,
alba, it smells like roses among
the garden's almost-summer smell.

She sits on the steps; they're hot
not too hot. She picks up her blue pipe.

Beside her the bowl
holds water gluey with soap
& drops of grandma's glycerine.
The pipe-cup breaks its disk of light.

Trying to be even & be slow
she bites on the pipe-stem.
Her breath steadies;
she blows out a bubble,
another, the two
float over the pansies
into the bridal-wreath bush
and disappear.

Getting married is like that.
Getting married is not like that.

SEPARATE, IN THE SWIM

(Temara Plage, Morocco)

Oiled and drowsy, idling in a sling
of turquoise cotton, you take the sun.

I stow my rings, cash, shirt, & frayed
cords of connection under your chair.

I cross bands of hot sand then damp cool,
to the waves rustling up
broken by the aim of wave, the idea
that picks up the water
and throws it at the shore.

Invading the invading sea, leaning to it
arms at an angle, I wade in slowly,
weight forward, leading with my knees,
soft-jumping in answer to wave-swell.

Wet to the hips I dive under
and swim turning in to pleasure.
The sea surges inshore. I surge out.

The seas alter me and alter after me,
allowing me a horizontal stride.
Armstrokes & legstrokes echo in my cells
heating the circuit of blood.

Each stroke starts a far drumming
clumping the kelp, helping
shells and rubbish decay into sand.
I press out a pulse (it will
throb back as another pulse) along
the sea-floor and the furthest beaches.
In this stretch of the Atlantic
the whole Atlantic operates.

．　．　．

As I ride, its broad cast evokes
my tiny unity, a pod, a person.

Thanks to the closure of skin
I'm forking the tune I'm part of
though my part is played moving
on a different instrument.
I hear the converse of wave-work
fluid in counterpoint, the current
unrupturing. I push: the Atlantic
resists so that I can push myself

toward a music which on this scale
is balance, balancing buoyancies,
able to condense me back out with it
having carried my will
forward awhile before
it carries me to shore.

You have slept.
You have taken the sun.
I towel myself dry.

THE STORY AFTER THE STORY

In bubbles to the elbow, on my knees,
I am washing children. You are laughing,
pleased to observe me at my mysteries.

Antoine & Will giggle as I sluice their backs.
My knees soaked by local tidal splashes
creak as I stand and towel two relaxed

bed-ready boys. I crib them, warm in their
soft shirts, & sit to eat a bruised sweet apple
as I nurse Chris and float on mild air

a story for everyone; Monique & Denis
settle on child-chairs; we are a tangle,
bitch and pups, in the oldest comity.

You like that less, leave us for the kitchen
to finish the fruit and cheese. The ample
story falls short on me. My mind itches.

Sighing & smiling Antoine drops to sleep.
Will lies awake, only his eyes active.
Monique trusts the story somehow to keep

mapping new ways home through more & more world.
Chris drowses. Will's eyelids lift up, lapse back.
Denis's fists lie in his lap, loosely curled.

I am willing them one by one to sleep.
The story wanders in its adjectives.
Chris's mouth clamps down, lets go, breathes deep.

·   ·   ·

Humming & murmuring I bed them all.
Monique tells a soft story, managing
me into mind with her as she too falls.

I rise in joy, ready, the child-work done.
I find you have gone out. A radical
of loss cancels what we might have become.

LIVING ROOM

The window's old & paint-stuck in its frame.
If we force it open the glass may break.
Broken windows cut, and let in the cold

to sharpen house-warm air with outside cold
that aches to buckle every saving frame
& let the wind drive ice in through the break

till chair cupboard walls stormhit all goods break.
The family picture, wrecked, soaked in cold,
would slip wet & dangling out of its frame.

Framed, it's a wind-break. It averts the worst cold.

AFTER THE PASTORAL

Just after dusk the tulips still show yellow.

This year my child goes where I can't follow.
My first is gone, the one where I began.
"Come back," I whisper. "Come in if you can."
Silence. I step out, ferocious with fear.
Dread enters my one, trance my other, ear.
The tulips fade. I drowse until dawn breaks.
My eyes open. I force myself awake.
Cowbirds crowd the ground wherever I look.

Where soft mouths taste the night, it sets its hook.

AUTUMN CLEAN-UP

There she is in her garden
bowing & dipping, reaching
stretched with her shears—
a Ceres commanding forces
no one else anymore fears.

The garden's not enclosed.
It encloses her. It helps her
hold her joy. (She is
too shy for transports.)

It helps keep her whole
when grief for unchangeable reasons
waits to gnaw a tunnel in her
to run around wild in,
grinding its little teeth,
eager to begin.

ROUNDSTONE COVE

The wind rises. The sea snarls in the fog
far from the attentive beaches of childhood—
no picnic, no striped chairs, no sand, no sun.

Here even by day cliffs obstruct the sun;
moonlight miles out mocks this abyss of fog.
I walk big-bellied, lost in motherhood,

hunched in a shell of coat, a blindered hood.
Alone a long time, I remember sun—
poor magic effort to undo the fog.

Fog hoods me. But the hood of fog is sun.

NON-VEGETARIAN

It haunts us, the misappropriated flesh,
be it Pelops' shoulder after Demeter's feast
or Adam's rib supporting Eve's new breasts,
or the nameless root of Gilgamesh.

Who am I that a given beast must die
to stake the smoulder of my blood or eyes?
Were only milk, fruit, honey to supply
my table, I would not starve but thrive.

But then the richer goods I misappropriate
(time wasted, help withheld, mean words for great)
would blaze forth and nag me to repudiate
the habitual greed of my normal state.

My guts delight twice in the death I dine on,
once for hunger, once for what meat distracts me from.

UNPLUGGED

Once, you were translucent; you stood between
me and the source; you tempered the light, became
the light I chose to see by. I have seen
by earth-light, straight, for a long time now. I name
the objects, powerful, that I have kept:
my bed, my laundry, my pantry, my stairs.

You took the valuables when you left.
Abandoning our old lamps and chairs
you unscrewed that incandescent choice of mine:
you my constant, the light-speed I saw by.
Disconnected you vanished. I define
growing things one by one, with my own eyes.

I miss, dismiss the lust for free obedience.
In natural light the world is immense.

BETTER

After a long wet season the rain's let up.
The list my life was on was critical;
reproach soaked it and infected my ears.
I hid, deaf and blind, my skin my hospital,
in the inoperable ache of fear.

Today the rain stops. I can hear! Trees drip.
They spatter & whisper as I walk their
breathing avenue. The wind has died back;
edge-catching light elaborates the air.

From the road car-tunes rush close then slacken.
I climb the green hill. There at last I reach
a figured stillness where no nightmares slide.

Green leaves turn inside out to grow. They breach
their barriers. I come, eyes wide, outside.

REMINDER

I am rich I am poor. Time is all I own.
I spend or hoard it for experience.
By the bitten wound the biting tooth is known.

Thrift is a venomous error, then, a stone
named bread or cash to support the pretense
that I'm rich. I am poor; time is all I own . . .

though I hold to memory: how spent time shone
as you approached, and the light loomed immense.
By the bitten wound the biting tooth is known,

though scars fade. I have memory on loan
while it evaporates; though it be dense
& I am rich, I am poor. Time is all I own

to sustain me—the moonlit skeleton
that holds my whole life in moving suspense.
By the bitten wound the biting tooth is known.

Ownership's brief, random, a suite of events.
If the past is long the future's short. Since
I am rich I am poor. Time is all I own.
By the bitten wound the biting tooth is known.

WE ARE IMAGINED

Time has expanded between us, like the spread
stain of a war we weren't fighting in.
Neutrals shed history. We have shed
the gentle sense we made together then.

    I suppose routs of soldiers have occupied
    the house we left unplanned-for—
    raw troops, more tired than terrified.
    Their shit and cook-fires star the floor.
    Our garden's gone to seed. Our valuables
    we left locked in a bomb-cellar at the foreign
    bank. We, who are now one and one and never
    there, will never see it again.

    I suppose one night a soldier
    finds by flashlight the necklace
    you gave me. He pockets the blue stones
    to send to his girl back home
    well out of the war zone.
    He wonders whose it once was.
    He guesses, that is, at us two.

    I suppose his idea imagines
    that the war will end & we
    will mourn the necklace missing it
    while he'll smile at his bride
    rounding to pregnancy,
    the beads' blue-violet shadow
    above her cotton summer dress;
    and he will caress her arm & tell
    about the war including
    the worst of it, & confess,

and she will cry for him
but not make a fuss.

And they will chat & imagine
something compensatory
happening for us.

III

The Split Image of Attention

THE SPLIT IMAGE OF ATTENTION
(illuminated MS, Trinity College, Dublin)

Saints in the *Book of Dimma*
deserve their double-rainbow eyes
for seeing form & structure,
skin & skeleton, both
at once. Great
lovers of instruction,
mouths empty, they tip
their earlobes forward
the better to lock in
the learning
inviting it as it enters and is intimate
with their diamond-cut holy
double-bolted ears.

I look to the next page where
having taken as their text
a wordshape so precipitous
it makes crystals of their tears

they divine the structuring
nature of genesis

& their eyes irradiate
on their own   full
of fear   hearing the meaning
of shooting stars.

READING A LARGE SERVING DISH

(Greek, ca. 400 B.C., Chicago Art Institute)

Persephone white-faced
carries her vegetal cross
on a stalk perpendicular
over her shoulder as she heads
up & out for home
& mother, her brilliant mother.

Closing, Hell's house lies behind her
(and, of course, opening, before).

Four creamy horses
implacably processional
are hauling her chariot
—red-orange on black ceramic—
toward her spring turn of sky.
They head for the edge
of the dish of plenty that honors
her style of exchange (exile for exile)
and her game of rounders (no winners, no losers)
her poverty her plenty.

    The dish itself is Demosthenes' age.
    Its suave lines issue its invitation,
    open-ended, a strange attractor.

    It tells you it will
    if you eat from it teach
    your deepening night to brighten
    at the depth where no gesture
    is straightforward or false,
    and you do not need to expect
    you can rise beyond suffering.

SKIMMING RAW FOLK MATERIAL

The tale has bends in it. What can it mean
that he leaves on a quest for a talking horse

but comes back with a princess? In between
she gives him falcon-power, but remorse
starves him since he won't kill small game. (He'd feast
if the hut on chicken-legs hopped a snow-hid course
twirling before him through the woods.) He runs east,
west, sleep-deprived till he finds the last word
for sleep, but forgets it when a wakeful beast
proves to him his mother tongue's absurd.

It's about what all stories are about,
the bargain they offer or deny the heart:
to get home, leave home; pack; at dawn set out
on a trip dusk closes where it started.

ANALYSIS

Analysis prefers a mountain lake
without tributaries to account for.
It can't stand random splashing, can't just take
its clothes off and jump in. Its designs score
by degrees: first it looks, till it seizes
a sense of the whole; then it stares some more,
till the rippling surface stills & freezes.
Its bubbles flatten hard and rim the shore.

And now analysis cuts the ice to bits,
tens or thousands, each a telling device
flashing "lake" in part-song, true in how it fits
the cutter's visionary set for ice.

Patterns lapse in a bliss of signal mist
which concludes in the swim of the analyst.

BIRTHDAY

(for Rosemary Deen)

In for the winter, your Christmas cactus
shouts "Rose" & shoots its flame-sleek flowers out
in doubles at the end of each dark stem.
I can't copy such plenty. But I can
proclaim how well its structure celebrates
the lived poetic all your born days state.

When in thin winter you let summer state
its essential green by heating for us
jars of basil couched in oil, we celebrate
earth work sun work your work, opened out
when we most want freshness, in rites which can
retrace the tides of summer time must stem.

Autumn is inward. Wild buds sleep in stem,
rapt secret in their generative state.
November sends you in, with all you can
hold of harvest. Fruits you serve to us
you save in seed, too, then sort the seeds out.
Identified, they concelebrate.

That analysis is ours to celebrate.
Grain by grain you loft seeds into system
as in sonnets the ripe-dropped thought springs out.
Labeled, seeds shape the form their nature states.
You, general & scrupulous,
recast the particulars until we scan

the song-score of the year, because you can.
Gourds to seeds, words to poems celebrate
new places you flag as common to us,
their nature prized by so apt a system
we enter it like a long-lost mental state,
and dump our own sacks of odd fact-bits out.

. . .

We count on you. Laughing, you'll figure them out.
Elements, caught quick—as you always can—
flash-melt old grids down to a fluid state.
Fact-bits, basil, cactus, we, concelebrate
change as the blossoming source of system.
We breathe the green we eat. Time swims in us.

You flower for us flaring out from a stem
whose perennial seed-reach can make fall state
the final primal cause you celebrate.

ENDOXA, OR, REPUTABLE OPINIONS
(Aristotle, Bakhtin, T. Berry)

The tailor's sophist power grows
till young philosophy speaks, and shows
the emperor has no clothes.

Dialectic's spiral spins
beyond mere opinion, to propose:
the emperor's skin
is the emperor's clothes,
the dress the emperor's always in.

Boy Aristotle mapped these minds:
"What philosophy knows
and dialectic probes,
no sophist can find."

I unlike Aristotle watch
the world I reach disclose
what dialectic misses:

where I live is shiftier
than that fictive emperor is.

There is no cosmos,
just a cosmogenesis.

AROUND A BEAUTIFUL THEORY

(at the Getty Museum, Santa Monica)

I
Answering warriors
the washerwoman at the river, glancing
down the morning current
toward a bloody afternoon, said,
"I see red. I see red. I see red."

death sentences
instances of truth

& here in the hurt world
whose denials root in the soil
of the fear of dying,
the True rushed back to me from exile:
 Blood lends us a life-line.
 Death ends that lending.
 We shall die. We can say that's true.

But wait! to leap
(like a new hermeneutic
with antic old tricks)
from True to Beautiful
can't be done. It's
too dull, idle,
irresponsible, and unpopular.

2
Last week in Santa Monica
I almost got a grip on it.
If I'd been credentialled & dressed right,
an attentive Getty curator
might have let me hold
 for a minute

round in the round of my palm
out of its lit niche
the rock-crystal figure
whose attributes are love
(Aphrodite Artemis Is/
is) rising from trans
parent seas, her antecedents
undefined primitives
doubtful of access

yet she always is always the one
in whose hand we are already held: love.

3
It's only an artifact. It only looks
lit from within.
I'd have given her right back.

The hand is blind.

It's OK that the hand is blind.
Weight's what my hand wants,
the rosy body readable,
its density held to be brilliant,
its language of feeling
tactile, not a crack in it.

Erasing mis pelt joylessness
it writes the text of the beautiful
love we subscribe to
when accurately read.

Let it speak, and it speaks
an embodying beauty
so quick it can re-mind
the loved dead (their everydays dead)
as they (their beauty resisting

obliteration) are smuggled back in
through the vent the little beauty opens
to air the beautiful they were for us.
Re-membered, their presence gleams,
their absence unaccounted for here,
where fear of the beautiful
roots under the roots of fear.

Uninstructed, empty-handed, I can't
account for the commonly beautiful
        gardener washing the lettuces
        busdriver close-shaving corners
        teenager waiting on tables
or the para site panache of any joy

4
but look, I hold them harmless
in the turnkey question of the gap
the statue makes. Unearthed
she is giving herself airs,
ordering, "Use your eyes.
See. See. See."

Quiet, on her bright shelf, laid bare
she comes as love's summoner
tumbling in the lump of quartz.
The very track-light is beautiful.
Alive in it, curator,
I give myself airs

TWO QUESTIONS

(for E. Coleman, L. Ferlinghetti, E. Fontinell, G. Mally, D. Yezzo, all men of good will and sometime armed forces)

I

Dropped
brilliant
in such windrush he
can't scream
he's moving too
fast in the pitchblack
falling his
parachute hot buckles & charred string

he is on fire he hits salt
water, goes out   as he
goes under. It chokes with
him in his throat,
that shout.

Fire, the flare human, the
body of burning plunging,
shot star sea-quenched:
. . . fifty years on fire in my mind.

Second hand. Dreamed, dreamed,
a silence of scream, heat
into cold, extinguishing.
Waked by, wept for, guessed at,
an ignorant dream, dreaming those
who flew to kill again toward gunfire
flew killed flew killed flew   But he
burned, that boy, my age, Lt. Little,
prayed for in my parish monthly thirty years
till his mother died; who else would remember?
His lovers at then twenty-one
have long loved others. Only those

who made him up out of anguish
ignorant among war news remember
what the order of murder made.

2

Wasp & osprey flee our ring of discord
but now & then—as if some beast were fat
& we winter-struck with hunger—
we close in on it flourishing weaponry
and war makes meat of some.

In their poor young butchers
otherwise virtuous   it taints memory
with ownerless bitterness.

Our catch-basin cities swirl with blood
until—some larder stocked—we stop
come home   wash up   and restore
peace as if there were no war.

If slaughter always alters our memory
if brutal mistakes are fatal so far
& if I—no Amazon, no Lysistrata—agree
no life is free of brute fatality

what is a safe childhood for?

of what is war the history?

A DETERMINED PRESENT

Chance as it maps
the next necessity
steps her, step by step,
as if she is free.

Often enough, she finds herself
where she never chose to be:
in winter, under the prickly
branches of a Christmas tree;
or, come summer, thirsty
far from the general store
at a picnic table in New Hampshire
outside the local mental hospital
named Gethsemane, originally.

MOVERS AND SHAKERS

The Round Barn vaults a floor blessed
by the prayers of feet, a music threshed
by steppers ascending into long forgetfulness.

When winter lasts too long the prisoner
is tempted to become her own cage.

Though it dine on its own self,
for a tadpole
frog is heaven.

The architect of frog is damsel-fly,
a mortal/vital alchemy.

Vein and artery vital and inimical
collaborate in capillaries—
take exchange, give thanks.

Independent (in that best dream) all take
their time, to enjoy each other's company.

Summer caucasians tan and enjoy
a bronzed indifference, pretending
it eases the longing for equality.

Ice since autumn, sun eases its edges and
the brook starts a spring conversation.

IN FAVOR OF GOOD DREAMS
(a rann)

Memory,
hum wordless images, be
tuneful color for these dreams
whose greywashed streams greywash me.

In sleep-sprawl
my rare knives are hospital
not sexual; what they cut's
not mythic but surgical

error out,
banning the disease of doubt,
forcing steely discipline
to thin-slit my skin without

cruelty
or joy; knives act craftily
in inert flesh gone dumb.
But lovers come clumsily,

carefully,
carelessly, most patiently
together. Seek for me those
uncut roses, memory.

PRE-TEXT

for Douglas, at one

Archaic, his gestures
hieratic, just like Caesar or Sappho
or Mary's Jesus or Ann's Mary or Jane
Austen once, or me or your mother's you

the sudden baby surges to his feet
and sways, head forward, chin high,
arms akimbo, hands dangling idle,
elbows up, as if winged.

The features of his face stand out
amazed, all eyes as his aped posture
sustains him aloft
                    a step a step a rush
and he walks,

Young Anyone, his lifted point of view
far beyond the calendar.

What time is it? Firm in time
he is out of date—

like a cellarer for altar wines
tasting many summers in one glass,

or like a grandmother
in whose womb her
granddaughter once
slept in egg inside
grandma's unborn daughter's
folded ovaries.

FOR DJUNA BARNES AS JULIE RYDER

Jacobean savage, hurt while she slept,
words hide the healing secret her life kept.

Her first raw love-letters stay housed with her
all her life. They are from her grandmother.

In dream or in terror her father's mother,
cross-dressed as a plump impresario, beams.

A thread trembles. She falls back drugged with sleep.
The spinner backs away to doze, replete.

Where are you?   silence   *I'm leaving*   fear
I'll fall outside the sky   *You can't lose, dear.*

As its skin is stroked the iris opens
to pleasure in whatever weather happens.

Where are you?   Here love here.   Rapt.   *I teach
the body of joy no body may impeach.*

In the same old fear-dream, new breasts cold,
she buds (age 90) in grandma's buttonhole.

Hark to the measurer: "Bad-Good. Once-Now."
Liar! the once she loves her in is now.

Her tongue forks from her gum the last remaining
crumb of burnt-cork mustache. She swallows the grain.

TAKING THOUGHT

"Tom broods," Grandpa said. His genial brother Tom
gave me wooden dolls, sister-brother twins
from Switzerland. He danced like a charm
and could walk on the river from Brooklyn
to Manhattan in ice-stories he told.
He looked bigger when he brooded. His blue stare
took up the whole room and turned it cold
as he sat, not talking, in his leather chair.

Grandma, longing to bring him out of it,
cooked soup, bacon, coffee, for him to smell;
she sat close across from him and talked, as if
she were two people, saying his part as well
(she was famous for help, in the family)
till he smiled. He smiled like a statue set free.

IV

Explorers Cry Out Unheard

EXPLORERS CRY OUT UNHEARD

What I have in mind is the last wilderness.

I sweat to learn its heights of sun, scrub, ants,
its gashes full of shadows and odd plants,
as inch by inch it yields to my hard press.

And the way behind me changes as I advance.
If interdependence shapes the biomass,
though I plot my next step by pure chance
I can't go wrong. Even willful deviance
connects me to all the rest. The changing past
includes and can't excerpt me. Memory grants
just the nothing it knows, & my distress
drives me toward the imagined truths I stalk,
those savages. Warned by their haunting talk,
their gestures, I guess they mean no. Or yes.

WINTER

I don't know what to say to you, neighbor,
as you shovel snow from your part of our street
neat in your Greek black. I've waited for
chance to find words; now, by chance, we meet.

We took our boys to the same kindergarten,
thirteen years ago when our husbands went.
Both boys hated school, dropped out feral, dropped in
to separate troubles. You shift snow fast, back bent,
but your boy killed himself, six days dead.

My boy washed your wall when the police were done.
He says, "We weren't friends?" and shakes his head,
"I told him it was great he had that gun,"
and shakes. I shake, close to you, close to you.
You have a path to clear, and so you do.

ALL WET

Underwater, keeled in seas,
zinc the sacrificial anode gives
electrons up to save the sunk hull from salt.

The carving of salt water skirls out beaches
where each wave fall can push softly, a long curve in.

Rain widens the waterfall till the stream
slows, swells, winds up, and topples down
onto lilypads it presses forward on their stems.

Carp drowse among stems sunk in the park lake,
their flesh rich in heavy metals. Eat one and die.

A drip from the tap hits the metal sink
& splats into sunlight, cosmic,
a scatter of smaller drops.

One raindrop on a binocular lens,
and a spectrum haloes the far field.

Haloes dim the form they gild but
by its own edge each object celebrates
the remarkable world.

Personal computers make dry remarks, demanding:
Tea, wine, cups must leave the room.

We're all the wine of something. His Dickens act,
her Wordsworth murmurs, expressed
juices still in ferment when their old children read.

. . .

Bones left after dinner simmer down into juices
to make a soup rich as respect or thrift.

As if making allowances
for the non-native limbs of swimmers,
water gives way as I spring into it.

SNAP SHOTS

From the hill road the golf-turf's a postcard
of canny grass. At its hardwood edge
3 deer stall ready to enter or to run.

Curves of clouds run parallel to low earth
where odors flow vertically, circularly.

Echoes of thunder far off flow over fields
& die away under trees that shed
the veiled sound of working leaves.

Late-fall sounds of grass stopping growing
tickle the hearing of ants & crickets.

Insects hear through plaques of listening.
They talk with fictive feet
or sing with greenish wings.

A greens-keeper rides the fairway
back to the first from the eighteenth hole.

West on 18th an old waif
crumples himself throwaway in cardboard.
Pray don't pry. Footstep past.

Night past, the deep-freeze people unbend & stand
to stir the blood puddled in their extremities.

They keep their place
with one shoe on top of their flat cartons
to signify, "Mine, okay?"

                     .   .   .

Mine says the mole in the parking lot. Mine says the flea on the
    mole.
Mine says the golfer teeing up. Mine? I say, make mine
    spring.

UNDERBUTTER

This house has three entrance-ways.
Water flushes its hidden places.

Sun-flush slides rosily off the wall. Dusk dawns.
Cats want out. Deer nose out of the woodlot.
Bats scour the near air as it cools.

Wheel-house: the house rides a cooling land-mass.
Oceans hiding desirable continents
flank it. The round earth turns it as it rides.

Its flank turned to the flank of the hill, the dog
turns off the vista and sniffs at fresh grass.

Angels fly into the fresh vat of cream
& suddenly it's butter.

Sudden awe sudden dread: the visible
fontanelle just under the scalp
of the delicate new-born head.

The delicate tip of the window geranium broke off.
The root-threads pop out a strong bud, lower down.

PERSEPHONE, PACKING

"I have two lives that change like dreams.
One dream, always the same,
connects the two, about to come
or able to be about to come true.
In it, I am of
my mother, or rather she
is the above-ground tree,
with me her underground and stemming
source, her feeder-rooted downtree,
whose work depends on the rock
below top-soil. If
(freezing & melting, freezing again) earth
heaves, I do not heave, but sing myself
back down warm with a story for
our sameness, our channels systemic
& open to each other's benefit.

This is just a dream
or underwater mirror
not what it would have been

if, the one facing the other,
we had ever stood still
and seen each other's face,
how gradual they are,
historical.
        As it is,
the dream goes dim with longing
to be the cause of light.
It wants to wake me up.

              · · ·

It can't die out or blossom;
it's stuck in autumn, impacted,
its roots spidered, replete,
like the bulb narcissus,
like daffodil & hyacinth in bulb,
or tulips, daughtering."

FESTIVAL OF BREAD

(dans l'Ain, la France profonde)

Suicide, in a village of forty heads,
is loud language—mythic but personal.
This year's been hard. A father hanged himself
in time for New Year's. Now at noon on May Day
the son's found drowned, sand in his redblond hair
facedown in the shallows of a river
a fox can walk across, head above water—
a week before the hay comes in. Despair's
not a word they use. An aunt's come to stay.

The village has restored its old twelve-loaf
common oven, for a Bread Festival.
Tourists find old-time comfort in good bread.

The widow shoves her night-time self aside,
kneads silence down into dough, and lets it rise.

FULL MOON, UNSTRESSED MEASURES

(for Marilyn Hacker)

O moon, we are not Sung Chinese. We
lack the court rhythm of moon-views.
In our tradition
the moon is for metaphor
but we speak to your presence
measuring our words.

O moon we are women & travelers
whose obedience you will not
(among all earth's obedient)
have noticed. Though it is real
we are small.
We are friends,
maternal not virginal.
We stand for praise of your part
in our children.
Shine for them, far from us.
Remind them of, call them
to themselves by,
gradual intervals,
turn and return.
Regulate them lightly.

We praise your recurring,
the continuous bass of your
luminous groundwork.
We hear you. Your melodies ride
the beat of the silence between
your old light & new light.
We listen like percussionists.

In ten strokes of your pulse
a healthy woman makes a child.

. . .

Tonight you climb to your height
flamboyantly, angling
light lost to us back to us.
      Below this terrace a gorge fills up
      with mist you filter through,
      until it shows you off. Olive leaves
      break your shine into small ovals
      which the wind stirs.
      In the woods opposite,
      two dogs salute you,
      guttural, and are still.

You have been here before,
keeping faith with being
beautiful. You are used to
the attention of women your phases recall
to their generative pleasures.

To those who have walked on you, you pay
no heed. You spared them your stones,
your power untrammeled.
Your gravity orders
the meadows and mines
of the subsurface sea,
their gossip & converse,
their wave-carried rumors.

We speak plainer to each other
with you here. We can name what we fear
for our children, what discord.

At home in our street-canaled cities,
where natural beauty is human or sky,
our harbors reflect your behavior.
Our calendars mark the nights
you will signal to us.

We incorporate your cycles
arranged for two melodic lines:
short dusk/dawn, long fall/spring.
They move us to desire
the high view you hold available
above your repetitions. The lilt of it
rinses duplicity out of our ears
& lifts us. We triple the rhythm
by adding the pulse of our words,
in which the human things we shuffle
are exalted, and, exalted, ride
a tune uncramped and ample,

as natural as our light breathing
and as complex.

OCEANS

(for William Cook, drowned in Maine, and for Roy Huss, lost in Indonesia)

Death is breath-taking. We all die young,
our lives defined by failure of the heart,
our fire drowned in failure of the lungs.
Still planning on pouring the best ripe part
of wines our need or grasp has sucked or wrung
from fruit & sun, we're stopped before we start.
Taste like talk fades from the stiffening tongue.

In reach of what we've wanted, our hope is strung
toward closing chords of accomplishment; we
grip ourselves.
                        Cut off we go stunned, raw
as a land-child brought out to see only
ocean all the way to sky. Shut in awe
we wrap our secret in us as we die
unsaid, the deaf objects of good-bye.

FOREIGN CORRESPONDENT

(for Margaret Fuller, drowned in shipwreck just off Fire Island, July 1850)

Margaret, always at Fire Island
I swim with you in mind,

you afraid of the sea
you ended in and as—
your neckbones chalk,
the lime of your kneecap
gone to the lobsterclaw,
and in the buoyant embrace
of saltwater, your blent chemistry.
When sandbars shift on the seafloor
they disturb your locked sea-chest,
its lumpy key, the victory medals
of your husband whose luck
fell just short of this shore.

Gothic at fifteen, I liked to pretend
I might find your lockbox
and dove and dove to explore
off the beach where storm-force sank you
and the bubble of your hope broke free
drowning your politics in metaphor.

I still pretend to sense you here, no ghost,
my elbows & nose out in the air of your urgency.

As the undertow makes itself felt I gulp breath
and swim harder against your destiny
riding the slipstream of your working changes
groping for the good inshore current,
my thoughts flawed but full of your prose
eager angry speculative.

. . .

A kickturn, & I check the beach-line
you likely saw flare-lit. Now
the summer waves are soft
as your lake-summer days
with Indian women, you gesturing
toward the amity common among them,
holding a baby, a shawl,
your account of this long out of print,
your histories drowned in their only versions.

I peel myself upright
out of your warm element
and walk the sand where Thoreau
all that next day went rushing
scouring the seawrack for signs,
your reticule, the sea-chest
of manuscripts, a word
from any who'd seen you.

Staring without finding, he began
to be able to think what to do,
could do nothing, gave up, and
crossed back to the mainland
over the water
glittering in windwash
transcendent with afterstorm.

AGAINST THE DARK, NEW POETS RISE

(for Christopher Baswell)

Look up, there's burning going on,
exploding old stuff into new.

It's never winter everywhere,
so the sun says. So says the sky
where, dot-to-dot, Giant Orion
hoists a winter warning
up the north of night.

Bellatrix sets out her flares
above the fires of three Magician Kings,
saying: Because we whose lives
are drawn take time burning,
summer gone is summer coming.
Look up,

look, cupped
in the blaze of the Barnard Buckle
flames of interstellar haze embrace,
sight of their nuptials given to us
by a nest, behind them,
phoenix, of generous
growing hot young stars.

WHAT THE WORN RHYMES FOUND

Wherever she looked today, she looked too late.
Everything had been a poem for years,
even the fleas, even the bread-plate,
even the anonymous funeral's tears
in face-lines they shone to illuminate.

Only the tough unsayable remains:
why she lied to them, what long lies she told,
and that is a story of such dense pain
she froze to forget it, forced it to go cold
long ago. Now & then, though, in her tested brain
the place it at last went dumb in
shows the jeweller a stain,
cyanide and gold.

CLIMBING IN BIG BEND NATIONAL PARK

This up-slope opens like Adam, and in
giant Eden the mountain's rib lies bare,
its arch gashed white, like Eve a possible
cataract spot split to its origin,
a splurge of stone curved like a pelvic floor.

Our stares falter, eye-shaped, elliptical.
We city people laugh to shrug off awe,
pupils awkward with these vast geographies.
We blink (quick curtain) then drink in what we see
with the thirst of the reach we climbed here for.

We stand above tree level. We are the trees.
We catch wind-storm breaths. Our branches claw.
We drink sky. It stretches us. We don't care.
We catch jokes & luck from thin tall blue air.

EVEN

I
Were there cliffs cupping Eden?
I think it so   just high enough
for the travel of shadows & echoes

Vegetal animal
Eden was nothing
Adam was nothing

> *Animal   vegetal*
> *he is on stage a while*
> *before he speaks*

> *From wing to wing*
> *air lifts and rustles*
> *The light is general*
> *a wonderful consonance*

                              Adam wakes present
                              in the present tense
                              to his present Eve

> *Eve comes to*

Adam was nothing
not even lonely   till
Eve came to
            listening

                              In Eve's eyes
                              Adam is faced

                    .   .   .

Each is the only equal
They stand definite
the same in their luminous skins
their faces regarded the same

                Adam is / Eve is
                nothing   much yet but
                by their same difference
                Eden is seen to be everywhere
                What they see is Eden
                            Being

Eve came to invent us
          invent audience
taking in hearing
she came to hear him:
        sponsa
        respondens

           the birth of responsible life

He would hear her
she would be there to hear

                With trials of consonants
                labials gutturals stops
                        out of breath
                Adam begins: Br. Sh. Th. Kr.

The names stick.
The air waits. Eden
fades   the beasts
stop short   The river
threatens to harden.
        Adam's skull
stammers & hurts

                Eve opens her ears

. . .

She is   listening

On the waves the whorls embraced
Adam came   to her mind
as the sound of Adam

                              Her throat aches

a great longing
"Ah," she replied

                                        "ah"

            o Eve is out in the open
            a toss-up of vowels & verbs

Her diverted breath informed her

                        loosening vision & interludes
                        fluency   silence
                        a diverse civility

            Aren't they something
            Both are the only equal
            and the speaking listener

Eden's creatures, eased, began flexing
out of their names their spines & joints
crackled & shone   acting in syntax
answering   her answering
                        flowering vines
hung fruited with stories

            Through each other
            microscope telescope
            they look at the garden
            Landscape enlarges them

．　．　．

The oxen lift their knees
the baboon flaunts its pink
the various frogs
touch the high pitch & low
of audible sound　　Their range
arranges them　　articulate

Syllables act on the two
who hearing say Syllable
—action　　syntaction
how touching　　what tact
Invented by listening
sound invents sentences.

The breeze drags fragrance through consensual intervals of air.

Confirmed by cliffs, their usual gaze
looked not down but across
neither upward but on the level
at Eden　　each other.
Journeys　　never occurred to them
even at evening
when the only Other often arrived
and they breathed in.

Together they breathe
that Other breath.

They breathe that in & out
they keep on breathing.

2

In a sift of ash in Wales,
at the bottom of a pit sunk
in the crucial chamber of a passage grave,
its stones cut & laid up dry

5,000 years ago, about, diggers found
and anatomists identified a small
bone of the inner ear. It is that of a girl
8 to 10 years old, in perfect condition.

Lost is found. Salvation.
I happened to hear of it.

If I can hear this
what may I not hear

Sight's the electric hunger, though sensual Blake
says hearing's the most intimate appetite.

Bird what do you praise Praise it
again among the juniper plumes
& silvered-blue juniper berrybeads

Your birdpraise rivers the juniper air
until I admit the incision of listening,
and self rising easily up off the river
evaporates altered into its liberty

3
Sundown, & under the afterglow
woods and fields fall still.
Hidden, the daycreatures drowse.
Nightcreatures step soft; rabbits go cautious
& the hunt is up for the unwary in-between.

Under the trees fireflies exclaim.
After dinner city people on vacation
hold hands, having been promised the moon
which is rising up a dark-collecting sky.
It is June, trees hold still, the breeze
holds its breath. I stroll out into the dim field
open to great horned owls, too big to fear them.

. . .

My mother & father are walking out
hand in hand in my mind of summer
into the shadowed meadow
crowded with flickering lights
in the Poconos in nineteen-nineteen
under their honeymoon.

He calls them lightning bugs, she laughs & says
Fireflies though the hotel receptionist
said there were glow-worms, how funny.

They do not plan to remember it all their lives
but they do. Haunted by silence, they do.
It wasn't easily talked of. All I know is,
neither ever saw again
such shining flying in every direction,
acres of low-lying air where wild sparks
pulsed silent in the dark. Until they died,
it would flare up in them at times.

He turned the talk to the lightning of storms,
listening to her fear & attraction; always
he answered around her to keep her if he could
from hurting, with her wit where he was tender,
or with slow tears if his wit spoke.
It got better after twenty years or so.
They found themselves
each in the other's power & lost dread.
He would or she would take turns
managing to dredge up hope
in rummaging just for luck
for heaven in the marriage
that was their Lost & Found.

      Write lost as cost;
      spell fond, spell fund, spell found;
      spell band, spell bond, spell-bound.

                        .   .   .

And as well, if you will,
spell promise, premise;
        ratified,
        gratified.

4
After judgment & the wet sacrament of slaughter,

greener than Eden, a shock of bliss to see
just past the stew & suck of reeking waters,
the earth ate sunshine under the olive trees.

Noah, his wife, their sons, their daughters
rushed to lower the gangplank. Awkward, long doubled,
unboxed & jostling, the passengers suddenly free
hustled uncoupling ashore to uncouple, suddenly free.

from SPRINGING (2002)

New Poems

OLD JOKES APPRECIATE

Up the long stairs I run
stumbling, expectant.
Impatience is hopelessly
desperate.   Hope
takes time.

Sort out the private from the personal.
Advance on losses at a decent pace.

"Aside from all that, Mrs. Lincoln,
how did you like the play?"

DRUNK & DISORDERLY, BIG HAIR

Handmaid to Cybele,
she is a Dactyl, a
tangle-haired leap-taking
hot Corybantica.

Torch-light & cymbal-strikes
scamper along with her.
Kniving & shouting, she
heads up her dancing girls'
streaming sorority, glamorous
over the forested slopes of Mt. Ida

    until she hits 60 and
    loses it (since she's supposed
    to be losing it, loses it).
    Someone takes over
    her sickle & signature tune. Soon
    they leave her & she doesn't care.

    Down to the valley floor
    scared she won't make it, she
    slipslides unlit to no rhythm,
    not screaming. But now she can
    hear in the distance
    some new thing, surprising.
    She likes it. She wants it.
    What is it? Its echoes originate
    sober as heartbeats, her beat,
    unexpected. It woos her.

    The rhythm's complex
    —like the longing to improvise

or, like Aubade inside Lullaby
inside a falling and rising
of planets. A clouding. A clearing.
She listens. It happens
between her own two ears.

ORIGIN

The skull or shell
or wall of bone shaped
with its egg advantages
does not advertise

the gardens it contains,
the marriages, the furies,
or the city it shelters
(clangs, clouds, silences,
found souls crowding,
big dank cans where things
putrify)

or the glade it hides
for us to hide in, where
—our lives eased open—
we drowse by the pond and wake
beside ourselves with thirst,
where (dipping the cup we find)
we get of necessity
a drink of some depth
full of taste
and original
energy.

The darling face,
the fragrant chevelure,
even the beautiful ears

on the shell do not
boast about the workplace inside.

They prefer to appear to agree
they are just along for the ride.

WHAT WOULD YOU LIKE TO BE
WHEN YOU GROW UP?

I

Here I am in the garden
on my knees digging
as if I were innocent,
gloveless in island soil—
     sandy, unstable,
     hardly soil at all,
     very sharp and mineral.

Planted to temper the heat,
this garden has trees & fruit trees.
After a stormy spring
it's a low-walled well of green
bouncing into blossoming.
Already it turns me
toward autumn crocus now in leaf,
chrysanthemum, feverfew,
white & gold after the pears drop.

It's at its best in winter,
free of me, as I imagine it—
its six wonderful places to sit
(next to the tarragon and sage,
under the dogwood for breakfast,
on a log beside the speedwell).

It has taught me
     planning which is essential
          is impossible.

Mistakes (bittersweet, honeysuckle)
come back every year
hugely bountiful. So do

the peonies, lilies, & daylilies,
& grandma's rampant rose.

  Dear garden of my making
  stuffed with my ideas & sweat,
  you are reasonable.
  Your pleasure
  is, like me, physical.

  So, behave.
  I can't keep counting on my fingers
  to make sure all your parts are on hand.

I head for the kitchen, to cook.
I have no other plans.

You were not what I needed after all.

2
The reason for the garden is
this rooming house, this tidy
body's heart, my minded body

where I now rent only
the attic regularly,
and the kitchen, on odd nights.

It is the shabby residence
or sidereal repeat
of recurrent astonishment.
And it has known in every room
the othering bliss of child,
my child, each child different
for each other's sake, each
blessing me blind,
tenant & ceaseless & tiresomely
teaching me

relentlessly
to reach joy by choosing
to love. I so choose, I think.

Only the rich can choose to be poor.
There must be something I can do.

I think I've got whatever I need
in the overhead compartment.

NOW THEN

For a moment I know
I know what can be known.
Error abandons me
breathing an air
of blinding candor.

Candid,
       elated between
rivers twisting through stone
I draw close to home
and am not alone
alone.

       Time outlasts the moment.
       Felicity goes thin.
       It loses translucence,
       fades to transparency,
       and faithfully
       its cleared glass makes
       the other side known.

DECORUM, REFLECTION

Horace, decorous,

glimmers reflected
watching her gestures, in
brazier-lit glimpses
over her shoulder.

He sees her ivory
(under his urging)
gleam in the opposite
mirrors, her mouth soft,

her eye-lidded eyes
twinned like the nipples
rosy and rising
below her collar-bone.

Pleased he is pleasing,
he is well-meaning.
Subtly admiring,
he knows her by name.

Oiled, warm, they soon turn
in to each other.
Business is business.
No longer chatty,
not quite done laughing,
lithe young Lalage
welcomes him home.

GHOSTS OF NARRATIVE

Exodus 4:24–26

I
In the stories that make us
      they wait mysterious
for us to sleep, & wake them
so they can change us,
cruising in currents of feeling
stirred against the tide.

Job's daughters turn up first
in good shoes, alert & able,
saying, "Did you hear that!?
Who does he think he is!"

Lot's daughters look up
and stop crying.

Dinah brushes her torn hair dry.

Deborah honeycombed
by the verdicts of her prophecies
joins them.

When we glimpse them again, each
tells another's story as her own
and then, together,
these fine young women laugh.

2
The Egyptian sprig
who salvaged Moses
from among the rushes
slips past us in profile
usable, useful, used.

. . .

Zipporah the Midian,
Moses's next alien life-guard,
strides mum
through the quarreling crowd
    that stumbles hungry
toward the Promised Land.

Moses is left in the lurch
    held back, holding back,
listening to history. There
Sara foresees him, Moses.
He is the mother of his people (us)

Mr. Elsewhere, hill-topped,
held, holding promise.
Sara grieves for him,

till she observes
how well off he is,
    is the only one to get there,
    is the Promised Land,
fertile and
extraterritorial,
    is, under his tongue, at ease

as an answer for her, Sara
our promiser.

    Her avoidance of angels
    is effortless.
    She calls Isaac to her.
    "A promise," she says, "is
    a promise," and they laugh.

METAPHYSICA

1.   *"Off the Rack," said Wittgenstein to Descartes*
What I'm in is a predicament
of course, and its course
is coarse, even in my eyes.

It's ill-cut, but fitting,
eccentric, ridiculous,
and just my size.

2.   *"The Subject Is the Object," said Wittgenstein to Freud*
The subject
rejected as suspect
objects to objects.

The object
rejected as abject
objects.

3.   *What He Said to His Friends*
I long to be
just
in time.

4.   *What He Said to Me*
If I'm not in the forest to see them
do the leaves of my forest glisten?

I cannot ask you to listen to
me unless you listen.

5.   *What He Really Said*
I decline
to decline.

QUICK IT CAN

Quick quick nothing
is broken, sweep up the mess,
bag it, twist it shut,
down the disposal chute with it—
a lumpy drop, bump thud
and out of mind, gone.

Turn the music up a little,
lean more on the bass,
get your equipoise back
with the drum-ripple
that your solar plexus
picks up as pleasure.
It'll steady your stride.

Oh and look out the window, over-look,
I mean, the area of this latest disaster—
let it go. Admire
the seagulls' sail, high
up the skyscraper thermals,
their sea cry, that mewl, their purposeful
surveillance of their world.

By the time they locate & grab
their next meal, the sack of bad writing
—bad, dim-witted, self-serving, sloppy, bad—
will be baled for dumping.
Don't worry. It won't come back to haunt you.
Change your pencil or try pen or
boot up some old stuff you still like
and work on that, if you can find any,
and I think you can; if it can't come back
to haunt you, though I think it can.

RODS & CONES, & THE STATUTE OF LIMITATIONS

"It's the averted eye
that catches sight of leopards
slipping through the midnight hedges
toward the house. Cones track
a stab of flashlight, but it's rods
whose illiterate vision of the night
grabs the shadows & explains
what's that beside me or what
glides up silent on me from behind—
rods, and wits. Yes
wits, as in, 'I had a feeling.'

I had a feeling you'd call.
I caught a glimpse of someone
in the rush coming out of the subway
and I thought, 'It's time. It's you.'

I was empty when we met, back then.
I know I owe you everything—Kafka, Mary Butts,
the way to wear scarves,
                to welcome brutal losses,
a talent for courteous silences.
I owe it all to you. A huge debt.

But I'm not frightened.
The doorbell's broken, the doorman
doesn't know you, the phone's off the hook,

the e-mail's unplugged,
I live on a very high floor,
and I've been sound asleep for hours."

WHAT CHANGES

1

Pliny's Encyclopedia says: Look
at all the window boxes, greening
on the skimpy sills of the city's poor—
Venus-altars! kept to speak
their longing
for the lost the country past,
their lost haven in the
springing world, their pastoral.

Put the bull to the ready cow.
put the seed in the warming soil:
farm work makes time for farmers;
farm work makes sense to them.

Necessity herself once housed in them
pitiless   and domestic
        as the ram or cat.
Only a growing longing is left to them.

2

Born urban, I locate the lost
where I last saw it, stuck stark
somewhere in a closet, shelved.

Morning sun smacks down
on the wind-hit greens
of my Noho terrace.

The beans survive by toughening
too tough to eat. Lilies stay short
affording just one flower to a stalk.
Plants so stressed live

feebly or freakily, even
the hardest to garden—
like the moonflowers, two months early
in their distress
blossoming a dozen a night
in their rush toward seed.
Their big petals
rip in the crosswinds but
their big fragrance circulates
attractively echoing
responsive life

lost to me, shrunk in my century
to the stutter of occasional balconies
or charming second houses
for Sunday-sized refreshment.

Vergil, Horace, Pliny, Theocritus
you didn't know the half of it.
Only the longing has grown.

3
I reach far back
to my grandmother's neighbor
grounding a boy desperately restless
    with a broken ankle,
keeping him busy like her,
telling him stories of soon,
handing him pails of seeds
to be sorted for next year's planting
within her sweet alyssum borders.

END OF OCTOBER

Leaves wait as the reversal of wind
comes to a stop. The stopped woods
are seized of quiet; waiting for rain
bird & bug conversations stutter to a
stop.
Between the road
and the car in the road and me in the car,
and the woods
and the forms standing tall and the broken
forms and the small forms that crawl there,
the rain begins to fall. Rain-strands,
thin slips of vertical rivers, roll
the shredded waters out of the cloud
and dump them puddling to the ground.
Like sticks half-drowned the trees
lean so my eyes snap some into
lightning shapes, bent & bent.
I leave the car to see where, lower,
the leaves of the shrubs beaten gold leaf
huddle together. In some spaces
nothing but rain appears.

Whatever crosses over
through the wall of rain
changes; old leaves are
now gold. The wall is
continuous, doorless. True,
to get past this wall
there's no need for a door
since it closes around me
as I go through.

ENTRANCED

1
For openers
any wall has doors in it.

Openers who want
a door (not for air
but for passing through)

open & shut it
forcefully, under
heavy pressure
from the atmosphere
outside.

The ideal opener investigates
those osmotic waterfalls
which infiltrate
doorless walls.

2
To enter the enclosure
of the garden
or the citadel

be door, be son
or daughter

to the dearness
of pleasure.

Exits are disclosure.
Making an exit
can unlock you—
the way entrances do—

. . .

to being
outgoing.

In verse & reverse
word and worm
both turn.

REAL ESTATE:
Kripplebush, New York

Having measured all the edges and seen
the dry-ridge landmarks of the property,
the salesman sells it (whatever that means).
Lawyers search title, convey deeds, decree
(whatever that means) it belongs to me.

I search too. True titles of this place are: Green
(evergreen) and Sky (fluency, canopy).

Low among leaves & needles, winds careen
with rushed sounds of water—and cross the sky
lisping like water changing its ground.

These deeds are unconveyed, and simplify
beyond all measure into moving sound.

I wake to walk here, walk to learn my bounds.

CRUDE CABIN, AT THE BRINK OF QUIET

An hour after the reminder
of a late September rain,

the cascade of water from the gutter
under the rippled tin roof into the water barrel

is over. Slackening to dripping
it's arriving at stillicide.

Planctum. Punctum.
Silences
        gradually
(drop) to next (drop)
lengthen,
        slowing

like the breath of falling
through thought toward sleep

like the pulse of the blood
between amorous play and dressing

like the pulse of pain
from sharp to sore during healing,

each drop's a signal event,
punctual, rendering a curve
declining as it turns

into silence that turns
into sound that, spent,
turns into silence again.

OUT OF WATER

A new embroidery of flowers, canary color,
        dots the grass already dotty
        with aster-white and clover.

I warn, "They won't last, out of water."
The children pick some anyway.

In or out of water
children don't last either.

I watch them as they pick.
Still free of what's next
      and what was yesterday
they pick today.

PATHETIC FALLACIES ARE BAD SCIENCE BUT
(on reading Susanne K. Langer's Mind)

If leaf-trash chokes the stream-bed,
reach for rock-bottom as you rake
the muck out. Let it slump dank,
and dry fading, flat above the bank.
Stand back. Watch the water vault ahead.
Its thrust sweeps the surface clean, shores the debris,
as it debrides its stone path to the lake,
clarity carrying clarity.

To see clear, resist the drag of images.
Take nature as it is, not Dame nor Kind.
Act in events; touch what you name. Abhor
easy obverts of natural metaphor.
Let human speech breathe out its best poor bridges
from mind to world, mind to self, mind to mind.

Yet, I admit the event of the wood thrush:
    In a footnote Langer (her book rapids-clean
    like the spring-water aired over sleeked rock)
    says she witnessed an August bird in shock
    when a hawk snatched its mate. It perched, rushed
    notes fluting two life-quotas in one flood,
    its lungs pushing its voice, flushing the keen
    calls, pumped out as the heart pumps blood,

        not in twilight or warning but noon & wrong,
        its old notes whistled too fast but accurate.

I read this drenched in bird-panic, its spine-
fusing loss all song, all loss; that loss mine
awash in unanswered unanswered song.
And I cannot claim we are not desolate.

ANTEPENULTIMATE

His work describes for us
eons of cycles of sun, drought,
earthquake, ice, calm,
& what they have done for us.
He earns his living learning
history & likelihood
by reading trees, sliced dead ones.
Me too but

with live ones, some of them
aged & hollowing, for instance
this pear tree
                          its elbow extending
one tall young branch
good for a decade or so
leafed out & flexibly
offering for ripening
its always ante-
penultimate pear.

AT THE BOTANICAL GARDENS,
UNIVERSITY OF BRITISH COLUMBIA

The lyf so short, the craft so long to lerne,
th'assay so hard, so sharp the conquering,
the dredful joy, alway that slit so yerne,
all this mene I by Love . . .

CHAUCER, *PARLIAMENT OF FOWLES*

Among the sepals crisping
where they strain apart to show
tips of blushy petals getting set
to push each other outward
into bloom, the bud
is readying
to extend its destiny.

The parts—the drinking roots
the arching leaves the gorgeous
come-hither blossoming,
the dredful joy in days of time—
maintain their efforts separately

though the loft & drift
of heavy odor from the heart
as petals open over it
proclaim their joyful unity
even as it dissipates.

AFTER-IMAGE, CORTES ISLAND

1
Decorated, and visible
by the blur of white
on its blackish package,
the bald-headed eagle is roosting

forty feet up,
hugging the blackish trunk
of the kingly fir tree,

sixty feet tall & still growing
in a straight thrust, its down-sloped
feathery branches pliant,
accommodating sweeps of wind by
lifting, sinking, lifting.

2
For a few days in summer
we live among eagles
                    casually
above a bouldered shore
among & under the Douglas firs.

Early sun races
to reflect along the water
a blinding stroke
that it shoots out

aimed here.
We must blink at it.

Eyes shut, the after-image
lasts in a retinal blaze.

It persists, pulsing
its edges poignant,
its colors changing
        chameleon lightning
        as its image goes into
        reversal, a swelling
        gold-edged diminishing

and after a couple of minutes
is gone like
remembering
unwillingly.

MY WORD IS MY BOND

"The neighborhood's older now
but it's still
a valley between vaults of stone.
Your corner grocery's gone.

When I walk there I've never left there.

I haunt the place
   where my honor died.

I keep
      a watching
            brief.

When you said
         Now do you love me?
I picked up my ripped shirt
and lied."

WE STAND OUR GROUND

As the earth comes to light,
so the mind to metaphor.

Remotely, they meet, those carriers.
Though either one be more, or less,
or nothing, current spurts
from thrown switch through socket
as they operate.

Wiry between them, and live,
I say my *I* and claim
the chemistry to speak
when words thrill & drive

—uncertainly, certainly—

fusing, taking liberty
evoking a reality that only
syntactic links guarantee.

As hands are to earth,
as eyes are to mind,
so is mind to memory.

STRONG, OFF ROUTE 209

Armstrong
is blowing the roof off
over the coffee-stop's
back-of-the-counter
radio.

She puts down her coffee
and rides with him;
the old woman wings with him
out, into her upper airs.

When he starts to sing
she shuts her eyes
and mouths the words
right on time
delicious

Louis Armstrong, summa
cum laude, young Lester
Young's young University.

IMAGINE THAT

May morning, and the child
in ironed overalls squats
to report to herself
on the poise of a silk-smooth
stone. She hefts it
in her right hand, shifts it
to her left, inspects,
strokes, tries a quick lick,

and sets it down, almost exactly
where she found it
                        in the yard in the dirt
                        in the grass in front of
the clump of fat-bud peonies.
She does not know the name, peony.

She does not know the name, stone.
She knows the stone by its gravity
its ironic taste its nameless
coloring

                        And after seventy years
will visit, again, the ready way
the stone settled back into place,
unevenly, not as it had been,
not exactly   but satisfactorily,
to lodge untended in her memory
among other long-lived perennials.

THE FIRST, AT THE LAST

1

I walk home from the hospital useless
playing word-games in my head. Well,
I hadn't seen you in fifty-odd years.
You're the same. And, given
the sacred space of the dying,
you are different.

Your heart's a wreck.
"Sorry," the doctor said
in a modified paragraph.
You, old pilot, ceiling zero,
not smiling, muttered, "Grounded."

2

Word-games say: the groundlings
are the under
standers, keeping
their heads up
so they can see
feetfirst the actors
on the stage. They know
the Ghost must be
Will Shakespeare by his feet.
Their feet are tired
when Act V opens
at the level of their eyes.
They wait for it, silent,
throats swelled reactive
for utterance, understudying
the action of the Act
as scenes accumulate, words
gone once spoken but

not lost on groundlings
grounded & rooted
(since Act I asked its question)
by passions that build in them
to take in, to undertake
the final Act.

3
All he undertook
goes under, under
the undergrowth he rose from
fly-boy, lovely
in his day.
All his clothes
—spruce suit & tie—
are underclothes
against ungrounded grey.
All his studies understudy
an unstudied play.

> *Under the under*
> *of what I remember*
> *we are both twenty*
> *and except with each other*
> *underemployed.*

> *It is summer.*
> *Under our butter, bread,*
> *summer's hunger satisfied.*

RAIN ALL NIGHT, PARIS

On the road home the tide is rising.

Riding the road-tide is dangerous
but it's not safe to stand still.
Hang on the verge & you drown.

I'm going along for the ride.
I may see more riders further on.
Drowning must wait till I get there

and who knows who might be waiting
with a flashlight, a thermos,
even a raft or canoe.

Uncollected Poems, 1946–1971

A VISIT

Fine bitches all, and Molly Dance . . .

—DJUNA BARNES

Come for duty's sake (as girls do) we watch
The sly very old woman wile away from her pious
And stagger-blind friend, their daily split of gin.
She pours big drinks. We think of what
Has crumpled, folded, slumped her flesh in
And muddied her once tumbling blood that, young,
Sped her, threaded with brave power: a Tower,
Now Babel, then of ivory, of the Shulamite,
Collapsed to this keen dame moving among
Herself. She hums, she plays with used bright
Ghosts, makes real dolls, and drinking sings Come here
My child, and feel it, dear. A crooking finger
Shows how hot the oven is.

(Also she is alive with hate.
Also she is afraid of hell. Also, we wish
We might, illiberal, uncompassionate,
Run from her smell, her teeth in the dish.)

Even dying, her life riots in her. We stand stock still
Though aswarm with itches under her disreputable smiles.
We manage to mean well. We endure, and more.
We learn time's pleasure, catch our future and its cure.
We're dear blood daughters to this every hag, and near kin
To any after this of those our mirrors tell us foolishly envy us,
Presuming us, who are young, to be beautiful, kind, and sure.

(1946)

SENSIBILITY

"Cloth of true gold or Midas cloth chemically interchanged
Is beautiful but cold, does not drape well,
Cannot lend itself to every kind of color,
Has almost no, only a subtly ugly, smell.

Plant fibres take color like a good bride her man,
Taken and taken, giving and getting her fill
But like brides' solo mornings are fragrantly cool;
Drape with archaic stiffness, are best if held still.

(Silk was made to conform to the magical
Ambience of worm to wings; its drape is vertical;
It's cool to touch, warm to wrap in; silk's special.)

Animals give us cloth incomparably whole, temperate,
Graceful, grateful in hand, keeping the weave and hue
We give it, better with use than when new."

The man who told me this grew
Anagogical nightmares dwarfed and askew
Under his pitiful iron bedstead, being mad;
But something of what he said was true.

(1947)

ST.-GERMAIN-DES-PRÉS:
Summer 1948

Crooked like all our ideas of ancient ascension
The abbey tower topples a little toward us in the haze,
Looking lightning-struck atop the quiet afternoon
Or perhaps visited by something toppling in other days.
Not now. Now grey, heavy, like a bank, the church
A house, is decorative and calm across the square,
Convenient for native weddings, funerals. From this cafe
It's handsome; it fits; smiling tourists recognize it there.

Now the ex-sergeant I've been drinking with has something to say:
    ("Don't go in there, kid, I been, it's
    dangerous, no light what I call light but
    inside it's gold all over and the gold is going.
    I mean gold air goes blowing, there's an old
    sky blue altar up there too, don't let that gold
    air blow on you.")

                                            (1948)

RITOURNELLE, FOR PARIS 1948

Down from the subtle grey Sorbonne and
Round the corner we come, to come
Into air moving, an altered air.
High, how bright, how the element of wings
Becomes something, swirls in
To some strong center near; it
Makes the peopled street stilly
Radiant: o here, see the magic
Magnet (it draws us): mimosa,
On sale in bunches from St.-Jean;
A sudden shudder of gold, a golden locus,
Branch-caught, a fog, all luminous,
Standing rush-bound in green tin cylinders
Before the sullen gay and selling
Paris face of the grey-cardiganed flower
Woman at the corner of Cluny.

With spring and the schools sleepless,
Alive and almost woman, I first now feel
Your intentions strike then dissipate
Marrying into my blood, sift drifting
Light-like everywhere.

The blown seen mimosa (we see it)
Blots up a shadow, all shadows, draws down
Light, is light's ripple, aura, echo,
Look, the little floral haze
Holds the whole tall air:

It blooms to illuminate
You in my bidden blood, you between

The Cluny garden and the flower
Woman, you in the human city, the human
City, you. And I take the banded branches
Brilliant from your hand.

(1949)

PRIVATE AND PROFANE

From loss of the old and lack of the new
From failure to make the right thing do
Save us, Lady Mary Wortley Montagu.
    From words not the word, from a feckless voice
    From poetic distress and from careless choice
    Exclude our intellects, James Joyce.
From genteel angels and apostles unappalled
From hollywood visions as virgins shawled
Guard our seeing, Grünewald.
    From calling kettle an existential pot,
    From bodying the ghost of whatever is not,
    John save us, o most subtle Scot.
From pace without cadence, from pleasures slip-shod
From eating the pease and rejecting the pod
Wolfgang keep us, lover of God.
    Couperin come with your duple measure
    Alter our minds against banal pleasure.
Dürer direct with strictness our vision;
Steady this flesh toward your made precision.
    Mistress of accurate minor pain,
    Lend wit for forbearance, prideless Jane.
From pretending to own what we secretly seek,
From (untimely, discourteous) the turned other cheek,
Protect our honor, Demetrius the Greek.
    From ignorance of structural line and bone
    From passion not pointed on truth alone
    Attract us, painters on Egyptian stone.
    From despair keep us, Aquin's dumb son;
    From despair keep us, Saint Welcome One;
    From lack of despair keep us, Djuna and John Donne.
That zeal for free will get us in deep,
That the chance to choose be the one we keep
That free will steel self in us against self-defense

That free will repeal in us our last pretense
That free will heal us
    Jeanne d'Arc, Job, Johnnie Skelton,
    Jehan de Beauce, composer Johann,
    Dark John Milton, Charter Oak John
Strike deep, divide us from cheap-got doubt;
Leap, leap between us and the easy out;
Teach us to seize, to use, to sleep well, to let go;
Let our loves, freed in us, gaudy and graceful, grow.

(1950)

ANNIVERSARY

The big doll being broken and the sawdust fall
all scattered by my shoes, not crying
I sit in my dark to discover o failure annulled
opens out in my hands a purse of golden
salvaged sovereigns, from floors of seas culled.

The dancing doll split in an anguish and all
the cords of its elegant limbs unstrung; I
stumble whistling; the bones of my skull
marvelously start to sing, the whole shell
of myself invents without peril and contains a court aubade.

I hid the dovesmall doll but something found it. Frightened
I gave the fire what was left. Surrounding, it mulled
dulcet over the melting jeweled two blue eyes.
That night our hearth was desolate, but then its stones
sprung flowered and the soaring rafters arched.

Now all the house laughs, the sun shouts out clearly: dawn!
the sea owes us all its treasures; under the soft the riotous
explosion of our waking kiss or gift, a stone plucked or shorn
free of gravity falls upward for us, slow, and lies there, quietly.

(1951)

PLEASANT AVENUE

Is in Manhattan
As only those who live there know.

Even the paper-store man is
Italian, Gio. To him even
The *Daily News* delivery
Truckman is mannerly: he
Stops the truck, brings
The corded bundle of papers
Unripped in & sets it on
The maroon-grained plastic seat
Of the dim lunch counter's end stool.
Gio sells and smokes cigars.
I like to watch him unwrap one and
Light it, as if he were
Watching himself.
He sells us mothers malted milk by the
Big tin, cheap, good for li bambini, si.
Men of power gather in his store at night.
My life is so small I feel no fear of them.

The grocer down the block
And the grocer's glowing
Wife shaped like an earth-minder
Sell no potatoes, but stand beside a sea
Of kinds of greens; he lifts from beside
Parsley-tied bunches of uncrimped parsley
A head of escarole, thrusting its gold-to-pale
Center part up from among its shaggy green
To show me, Ecce, I behold.
Glad for his sake I approve. I buy.
His wife allows of me because my babies
Love the very smell of her, & do not whine;

So, nodding, smiling, nervous, he lets me choose
Pears one by one after I sniff at each bottom
Blossom-end to see if they're sweet yet. So far
I have not bruised any of his fruit; in his store
Insofar as I am correct, I am permissible.

East five blocks is the hard
Ware store, outside the invisible
Italian enclave. Here are
Ricani, the laughers; for them
I always wish to be darkly
Much prettier, and elegant.
A capella two men search dueting
For the cement nails I want; I read
Roach killer labels, ant killer
Labels, mouse and rat killer labels;
I glance at kinds of traps and wish
My city had room for more of the less
Desperately alive (despite us)
Withstanders-of-man. But next door
The bodega lady's parrot blazes
Green and thrives!

Brakes on Lexington screech as the
Bodega lady scolds the knife-eyed gang-
Boys and they shuffle; she dares
Send them home to their mothers, sí
Sí sí sí sí sí sí, and they go,
Laughing. I'm not afraid of them either.
I have nothing to fear from them
Being I guess afraid only of the loss of love
And of hurting children. And so here
I have nothing to fear.

(1952)

"VILLE INDIGÈNE":
Afrique du Nord

Amazed in a garden shut high
In a cliff-caught city beautifully
Clear above the ocean and the sea,
High with a private love
You and I
Watch the processional one young Arab
Waiter come on attentive feet,
His apparent focus of balance our
Pleasure at his copper tray and tea.
Tea is at last not English but
Oriental, hot-mint, hot-sweet,
Indigenous to this graceful, mosaic-
Divided oblong of garden
Built to shelter princes at their
Ceremonies, built to shunt aside
The burnt-out streaming desert wind.
The royal garden's public now, though
Empty today of tourists save for our dazzled in-
Ranging love, high over the great waters,
Close within color-crowded walls,
Directly under the moving sky.

If we are visitors yes it is beautiful.
Madame est américaine? Madame est
Américaine. We all three smile. His formal
Waiter's garment is a blur of white
Against the semi-distant blurs
Of the big-clustered orange blue or
Violet blossoming vines. His robes
Are subtle. They move as softly as
The subtle walled-off wind stirs.
What inhabits him, however, is very still.

.   .   .

Against a blaze-blue sky blaze-white
Ungainly storks flash gloriously.
We're so high they seem to stoop to drop
Below us as they slide
In a majesty of omen-holding wing-spread
Into flight from rooftops level with our eyes.
When perched, they stand, contre-jour
Angled against all the sky, cut
Out, in an evidence of light. It is
Beautiful. Sight, seeing this, is satisfied.
The rampant streets crisscross, man-wide,
Up to here, violet-shadowed, beautiful.
With wild voices in prayer-shrill
Shadows beggars beautifully sing.
(It is God's act in you that they beseech.)
Flat white façades, mosaic-set, inscript,
Diminish, play back, enhance the sun
Into a beautiful distraction of tipped
Uninhabitable inhabited planes. Here each one
Is one; and is so most beautifully.

Even the root-of-violet black
Stinking ribbon of sewer guttering down the
Stone street sides is beautiful. Women
Columnar in white djellabas
Are each beautiful; at work, old, burdened;
Pregnant, at work, giggling together;
Little girls, quick at their work. Emancipated
Young women, buttoned into groundlength grey
Gowns by two hundred and twenty grey buttons,
Go gloved, masked, and slippered in sun red or
Cyclamen, fierce blue or green, with a chic
I must envy and a ribbonsupple movement
So beyond my angularity that envy flees.
A splendid people, beautifully moving in their
Beautiful city, courteous to quiet visitors.

· · ·

If we are not visitors but persons here;
If these sewers are my sewers, these sere
Exhausted men my men, these loneliest
Bearers of burdens my suffering women;
Their fairy-tale handful of lentils and old dates
My daily food; their ignorance mine
(As these are all mine and these strangers
All my blooded close relations though
Understanding's denied us and communication's
Impossible no matter what the tongue)
If I am these beggars and I am,
It is not less beautiful but my
Eyes are blistered by it
So that they cannot (love, keep
Me constant, us alive) (my peace is
I swear whatever where
You and I kissing stand
My head between your heavy hands
But we are now somewhere neither
Of us understands) cannot see. My eyes
That in this city cannot claim to see
Are beggar's eyes infected by this
Anguish, by these my
Deaths and marriages that I know
Are not ever to be
Known nor even
Wept by me.

(1953)

SAM REFUTED, RESPECTFULLY

Experience can't teach
What some are born knowing:
How comely it is to be,
Dreamily, what you're
Likely taken for—

But pray it teaches you
Never to keep score.

Few of us ever do
Get used to
Using as we're being
Used by (I don't)
Or used to seeing
That, apple or knuckle,
My is not I—
And only a saint won't
Now and then ignore why
Yours is not you.

Sam Johnson kicked
The stone of a stone,
Scraped his shoe
And his ankle bone,
And did not care
For he alone then
Had proved anew
Fair and square
That he alone to
Him alone was
Usable, true,
And there.

(1954)

TAKE ANY CARD

Take any card; if we agree
in the beginning that Elohim
can mean chosen then we may be
tranquil partners, unopposed,
uncommitted, gaming
as we join to regard
our cards how they cluster
like Eve's beasts come to naming
patient and innocent
urgently being themselves.

It is your turn. Take a card,
one at a time, one of mine,
  or any one,

and the Sun
explodes all over again
something crystalline happens
grows crowded with colors
goes blue-green and green;
somewhere too remote,
something too small to be seen
too lost and common in the deep
for the first time stops drifting
stands against the current
and moves of its own accord.

For these cards are words and unlock
possible tricks into becoming new
species of victories. We can afford
to allow words meaning, as a double gamble

because from the center of the circle
the whole pack is visible
and whatever card you take
may well be a chosen one.

(1955)

UNDER A ROUTINE PROCEDURE

Intelligent and kind often, hands, I can't count them,
About and upon me, now soar worse than dreams of scissors,
So many gifted hands gone huge with threat, the stars
Above the blood-haze making a warning pattern
In the divisive signals of an alien script, in a tongue
Dead as the downstreet tree whose roots, believe me,
Thrust and crawl deep. I too am obedient.
You are not admitted here yet.

> I say I fear I mean I love as I was
> Taught to fear and love and taught myself
> To exchange them both for you.

Relieved, you go. My thought seeks not that for comfort
But what once pleasured me; I remember such things well.
The harelipped anaesthetist leans dear and safe
Saying Hush, and Soon now. Someone else said Rest now.
Flashing. Arched above me. Bitter honey, insulted body.
You too? How much, which, of what some she did, do you
Do again at my quick yes? I'll never know. Revenge
Is in the vice versa, lover; laugh. I go under laughing.

At dawn knives and bottles are back on steel shelves.
I am back in the dim ward. I see the river. City boats scud.
We are simpler, Confucius, left to our urban selves,
Than the rain-forest people. Our temple
Has an altarstone and our altarstone sweats blood.

(1956)

ELEGY FOR ELIZABETH BLEECKER AVERELL

Abrupt as that blessing gesture you always made
when we met or went our ways, you've bravely fled
lonely as ever, and no more than usual afraid,
beyond us, Elizabeth, abruptly dead.

Outside, birdsharp songs sprinkle the seagreen grass;
small-leaved trees sparkle with birds in June light in sea air.
You're not kneeling here. This is your Requiem Mass.
We kneel; you triumph; your absence strains our sight.
Even later your sons, even grown, won't know how fair
how tall as bridal, vivid, their young young mother was.

Your hard grace, your handsome, hurt-taught
body that made much of much delight,
your flashing sun-bound head,
with you are dead.

In life you were merciful, loved
all degrees of subtle enemies, I
among them who sure I loved you did
not cherish you, and so now cry.
Elizabeth who living was courteous, was merry day by day,
glorious friend, befriend me beyond death;
show us who do not love or know love enough or go love's way
your now love without limit, please, Elizabeth

(1957)

GIGUE FOR CHRISTMAS EVE

"O woman, go gently; the beast is too old
To get up a trot when his belly is cold
—Poor creature; your own, if the truth must be told
Is as tight as a drum and how long can it hold?"

"I forgot him, good Joseph; forgive me, now do.
Go easy, poor donkey; I forgot about you
With my thinking we'd soon get some village in view.
Do you take your own time, now, the night is still new."

"Man dear are you mad?" the beast whispered aside.
"Far worse heels than hers have belabored my side!
Why, the woman you mention is God's own good bride
And I'm honored to have her along for the ride."

"Don't I know it," said Joseph. "But don't let her hear.
I say, 'Pity the donkey,' to capture her ear.
For herself she won't spare, and it's that that I fear
With the jog in this road that might bring her down here."

"O good Joseph! No wonder God made you her man!
Your respect for her nature's a pleasure to scan.
Now if God speed me easy, I'll run the whole span
And get you to Bedlam, according to plan!"

Well, the donkey's brave words woke twelve angels at least;
Four and twenty wings feathered the speed of the beast,
Till in Bedlam his burden was gently released
Just in time for the star that roared out of the east.

(1958)

TO FORBID GRIEF

Let her be. She ran a long way,
the hunting pack at her heels.
She ran from dawn to past noonday
before the pack at her heels.

The hunters never came near her
even at the last.
The end of desire dared her
and she did not let it past.

From dark to deep brightness gone,
from racing to rest,
we may not idly mourn
her whose brightness blessed.

Let her quit body be
whose light runs free.

(1959)

BECAUSE WE CERTAINLY HAVE NOTHING BETTER TO DO

Applaud the man of extremest scholarship
inspecting the mysteries of his fellow
subway passengers, whose habitual love lifts
his eyes from his book to take in the loud trip

Make a feast for the
tireless walker, the girl who paints
difficult pictures, who wanders so
strictly, responsibly looking and as
canny as the surest of the saints

Praise the anguished world that also holds
the ironic survivor the gentle
retired from business man
among his geraniums and neighbors,
an example of carefulness, gladness,
with his wife, both self-effacing,
in the supermarket, the polling-place.

Let us less wise than these
praise our power to
value their victories.

(1960)

SURVIVAL

Watching you strike worldly poses flirting
Excited with someone's arch French wife
While I converse about roses (Shakespeare,
Sappho, Eliot, Bowen, Yeats; they are in
Theophrastus; our gardens have aphids
Climbers and chromatic fugues) surrounded
By cups, coffee, cakes, the sleeping
Children's wooden toys, I seven months
Pregnant for the seventh time
Disappear

(1961)

SPRINGING

In a skiff on a sunrisen lake we are watchers.

Swimming aimlessly is luxury, just as walking
loudly up a shallow stream is.

As we lean over the deep well, we whisper.

Friends at hearths are drawn to the one warm air;
strangers meet on beaches drawn to the one wet sea.

What wd it be to be water, one body of water
(what water is is another mystery). (We are
water divided.) It wd be a self without walls,
with surface tension, specific gravity, a local
exchange between bedrock and cloud of falling and rising,
rising to fall, falling to rise.

(1962)

DIALOGUE OF NEMO AND PERSONNE

"Are you still nice to sleep with?
Do you snore?"

    "I'm so precise to leap with, that
    I'm twice as nice to peak with, and
    if I snored my every snort would make you, lady,
    like me more."

"But can I count on you to wake me
up on time?"

    "I've listened for your laughing in my
    history of gardens. I can help you
    list the whispers of the paths where dreaming takes you.
    You have only to agree and,
    I guarantee,
    yes, I'll wake you up on time."

"I'm visible here but I must be
anonymous along my periphery.
My garden shuts out no one, it does no harm.
But where I laugh, or whisper, you may not take stock.
I praise but do not need you. I've set the alarm.
I trust my own clock."

    "Though not proud you are not kind.
    Though I'll keep us in my mind, Marie,
    it may well be better for me
    that you go free.
    If you call that free."

(1963)

EXPLICATION DE TEXTE

Before spring began,
On a day ice melted early
The explorers' Samoyeds ran
Barking their laughing bark
Wild with February pleasure,

And came back yipping, nunciates:

They had found
What we all look for, treasure,

As if new-killed, a mastodon,
On a tilt of tundra
At the glacier's lip.

To it they had bayed their men proudly
Over the hard wet ground to show
The food mountain, the beast
Flash-frozen by surprise
A million melting springs ago;
Caught while cropping grass,
Its flesh still fresh,
Its great organs preserved perfectly.
With it were found
A fringe of benefits, dangling
From the Playland man-tall jaws:
Grasses now extinct and still golden
Buds and flowers of uncrushed
Marsh marigold,
Eons old.

Knowledge of these facts
Came to me painlessly

Via a *Reader's Digest* I read
Waiting on a wooden chair to see
The good J. Spivak, M.D.;
I think they mean:
That mammoths ate marigolds.
That dogs are clever.
That cold is a mystery.

I think they mean that despite
Odds and ills which defy even a keen
Diagnostician, despite
How readers digest how
Reader's Digest writers write
Up Life's Adventurous Perhaps,

Despite the lazy bowels, gin breath,
Wronged things, sick souls,
Murder, life at its worst,

Life came first, not death.
Despite you death
Life comes first

(1964)

THE CROW DRESSED IN PEACOCK FEATHERS

(Le Geai Paré des Plumes du Paon)

A peacock cast its feathers. A passing crow saw,
    And stuck them in among his own;
He swore their cock-eyed glory was home-grown,
    And walked out grand from crup to caw.
Real peacocks looked twice, and shrieking at his deceit
    Pecked, plucked, beaked until in defeat
He sought his own. The crows, shocked by his wild, wrecked state,
Thought him a foreigner and forced him to retreat.
    Some peacock crows circulate
On two feet, decked out in cast-offs of others' brains;
They are known as plagiarists by these ill-got gains.
    Enough said. I do not design
To cause these people any further harm or pain.
    Theirs is no business of mine.

(1965)

Translated from the French of Jean de La Fontaine, *Fables*, Book IV, 9.

A TALE TOLD BY ATHENEUS (VENUS CALLIPYGUS)

(Conte Tirée D'Athenée [Venus Callipyge])

Two sisters of ancient Greece both laid claim
To the finest, fairest rear of their time.
Which tail forged ahead? Which bottom's true fame
Topped? Which back was in front, which terce most prime?
A judge chose the elder girl's back matter;
Her finish was more fine and far matter.
She got the prize, and his heart; soon they wed.
"But the younger's sitter's not a smatter
Less meet; I'll marry her," his brother said.
It went so well, their joys were so perfected,
That after them a temple was erected
In honor of Venus Callipygus.
No other church— though I don't know its rite—
Could so, from head to epididymis,
Move me with deep devotion to its site.

(1966)

Translated from the French of Jean de La Fontaine, *Contes*, Part I, 6.

SYMPOSIUM HOLIDAY

Out of the sky I fell onto a little island
Ireland; without the Yes of the dame up from Gib,
and only nod's knowledge of Dedalus,

with a family name from Blake's day and
a bookish hope for heroines (bookish)
I dropped in on Dublin to my embarrassment.

Such treasure, such honor, such gold, so many
sea-sprung bright-spoken women & men! A woman
feels like a fooled harpy in the wrong pub, though.

Among those who permit themselves mutual courtesy
I came unready as a booted crusader crude on
the carpets of the silken King of Jerusalem;

they praised my step. With kind mockery they fed me
as if I were included. For desirable as well as
kniving speech is current among them, word-drunk or sober.

No Roman Law, no Industrial Devolution: God save us,
Joyce was right! the Phoenix lives—here!
I fear lèse-majesté. Someone, please tell the Irish

and make it stick, that their inability to imitate
their beauty need not humble them into pride,
nor their skill as vivisectionists.

(1967)

LAST RESORT

Admit me to the circle of light.
Out here the jackals snuffle
Where, I thought, lions ranged before.

I hear you coming. You unlock the door.
You do admit me, though last time
I left fast, left you baffled.

We make love and other excuses.
The air's rank. There's sand on the floor.
Between the walls a nestful of squirrels
Scuffles, mewing.

Jackals have their uses.

(1968)

"LUXURIA," DREAMBOAT

A small ship, but I can't board her—
where she sails the water's always cold,
choppy, its currents unpredictably
treacherous.

If I owned her, I might. But I can't afford her;
her price jumps ten percent each time she's sold
& she wasn't cheap when she belonged to me or you
or what wrecked both of us.

(1969)

HALF FULL

outside in
grief rage grey pain
bright pain
this is it the
worst cold spring
lost tired with too much to do
no time to fix the garden
no money
no friend
a pain in the gut
no good love
this is it the
bleak hurting year
I guess a lot of years
got me in to.

at noon of the long day
flat out taking time to catch my breath
under the butterfly drift
of apple petals I see the many
spears and heads of perennials
coming up! strong green
well I even see
lots of buds on that delicate
difficult old gorgeously
fireflowered
peony tree

(1970)

OUT OF THE NORTH: TWO VIEWS

1

    "Though I come
In this eagle's disguise
          dolent, dolent, soaring indolently,
          equating the weight of my body with
          the width of my wings so as to ease
          in a wide side-slipping spiral down
          toward the edge of the ring of trees,
though I address you
with eagle calls and cries

I am a giant really and you therefore
should love me since although you
claim you are a falcon, believe me,
you are a giant, too."

2

    "What I might well say
    will go unsaid
    though it whistle away
    inside my head.
Though you are eagle to my falcon eyes
And think us sons of morning in disguise

though neither nest nor monster made us
and although I know what you forget,
that we are a god's get; more, the space who begot us
never forgot us and never betrayed us,

I a falcon feel only the umbrel flow
of warm air mounting through this cooler hour,
streaming steadily up from the hollow of trees,
pressing under the wings of my venturesome body,
upholding your body and its imperial power.

. . .

What else I have to add
no one will hear from me.
What creature would not be glad
to scorn disguises, to see
with falcon sight your eagle urgency,
and to be what he seems to be?"

(1971)

EASY (2009)

———

for Rosemary Deen,
who is incomparably magnanimous

I

ALHAMBRA IN NEW YORK

for Rosemary Deen

From the kitchen corner comes
the low electric hum
of the five-petaled fan.
A stir of air reaches us
sweetly, as if it were fresh;
it governs our breath.
Our talk over dinner
could not be better even
were we caressed (if

we were as we were)
by a skim of air lifting to us
moonstruck off the long pool
at Alhambra years ago, there
where we are, as we know.

IF LIVE, STONES HEAR

Where there are two
choose more than one.

In the longing of silence
                    for sound
the longing of sound for
                        silence

makes waves. Are the winds
of outer space
an utterance
or simply the rush of change

are rivers under our ground
audible to stones and to moles,
or is their wet self-storage
self-contained.

Between silence and sound
we are balancing darkness,
making light of it,
like the barren pear
that used to bloom
in front of Elaine's uplifting
Second Avenue,
like the acacia trees
perfuming the rue d'Alésia.

FOR DENIS AT TEN

He is a serious boy, a visitor.
He sees how an orchard of apple trees
opens this oriole morning
into a fossil-rock field where cattle
would stumble were there no rose-tangled
old walls of stone to hold them away.
Whistling, he is the serious city boy
who, given a country mission, strides
down the cow path, juggling a greening
to shy at recalcitrant rumps. He knows
he was sent. He goes on his own;
he takes into account
cows, chipmunk nutters, cowplats, sky!
& stones, holding each other into a wall,
and a black snake sunning, and, sky.

Birds slip brightness in among nettles and thistles.
It is early July. He was sent to the brook
beyond the pasture, for watercress.
He goes there, whistling.
          Nothing reminds him of something.
He sees what is there to see.

THIS BRIDGE, LIKE POETRY, IS VERTIGO

In a time of dearth bring forth number, weight, & measure.

—WILLIAM BLAKE

Describing the wind that drives it, cloud
rides between earth and space. Cloud
shields earth from sun-scorch. Cloud
bursts to cure earth's thirst.   Cloud
—airy, wet, photogenic—
is a bridge or go-between;
it does as it is done by.
It condenses. It evaporates.
It draws seas up, rains down.
I do love the drift of clouds.
Cloud-love is irresistible,
untypical, uninfinite.

Deep above the linear city this morning
the cloud's soft bulk is almost unmoving.
The winds it rides are thin;
it makes them visible.
As sun hits it or if sun
quits us it's blown away
or rains itself or snows itself away.
It is indefinite:

This dawns on me: no cloud is measurable.

Make mine cloud.
Make mind cloud.

The clarity of cloud is in its edgelessness,
its each instant of edge involving
in formal invention, always
at liberty, at it, incessantly altering.
A lucky watcher will catch it
as it makes big moves:

up the line of sight it lifts
until it conjugates or
        dissipates,
its unidentical being intact
though it admits flyers.
It lets in wings. It lets them go.
It lets them.
It embraces mountains & spires built
to be steadfast; as it goes on
it lets go of them.
        It is not willing.
        It is not unwilling.

Late at night when my outdoors is
indoors, I picture clouds again:
        Come to mind, cloud.
        Come to cloud, mind.

ALONGSIDE THE POND

At the edge of vision
just short of sight
pond air shimmers pearly
unbroken ungated. Bright
mist engages me
silent unmediated.

When I turn
and look into it

I want birds.

FIT AUDIENCE

for David Rothenberg

(andante cantabile:
G sharp is not G natural)
Mozart and his starling
both loved to whistle.
What a pair.

Maybe for just this once
in our history of Bird
we can forgive the uncaged cager.
Our god-besot Mozart
bought it caged it kept it,
a fabulous singer
priceless but with useless wings.
When it sang out
loud, careless, impetuous,

Mozart's shoulder blades ached
        but he heard it sing.

HEAD TURKEY MUSES: A SOLILOQUY

"I spread my tail. You halt. I walk right by you, close up.
You let me. You'd better. You
have no choice. Back and forth
I edge you, by my walk.
Which is righteous. I've got
my game face on. I get
the angle of the beak just perfect—
up. It stops you short.
It pens you, helpless, to the spot.

I wait. A long beat. You freeze.
And I front you and you drop your head.
You admit my walk wins. I walk superior.
You? duck your little head, duck lower.
Good.   The ground feels warm.
My spurs get sharper every day.
I do not need to pen you anymore.
You know the score. You stay penned.
I am very busy. I am sentinel to
hens. I do them all. Not you. I do.

When crows scream Cover! I decide
to credit them. For your safety's sake
I fade my great red wattle down to pink.
When I take cover
everybody does.
You too. I keep an eye on your head (low)
and on your wattle (at all times, grey).
Geese overhead shout nonsense. I
gobble at them and they're gone. And you
are where I can see to you.
You stay. I let you stay."

ONE GRIMM BROTHER TO THE OTHER

"I've never lived inside the gingerbread house,
have you? I don't say I've never visited.
But never lived. I know I couldn't like to.
It's cramped and it stinks of being afraid.

Of what. Which am I. Who is she. Afraid
I'd hate to eat her & she'd make me sick.
Afraid she'd eat me last. First. Afraid
no sweet-tooth brat would fatten and be sweet
to roast & baste & eat. Afraid that once
I'd cooked them (& started a soup for stock—
full of oniongrass—I'd boil their bones to)
no more soft children would climb my candy fence
& nibble up the path to my cookie tree,
my door of chocolate (whose inside fear is
inside the fear inside),
                    afraid I'd catch my breath
& hear the swarm of mice squeak, 'Eat or die,'
and then I'd have to eat and I would die afraid."

PETER RABBIT'S MIDDLE SISTER

Mopsy, you were in your briar patch
birthplace the trustworthy sister, who ate
blackberries with cream & kept the floors swept.

You came back promptly when sent out to fetch
brown bread for supper, while your reprobate
brother adventured, broke things, got caught, leapt
free, lost his shirt, got scolded till you botched
your homework and cried for him till you slept.
Your grief was seeing him stand there wretched,

reproached for his deeds. Not he, you, wept,
your chest hot, your heart fast in the thorned clutch
of your hedge-hemmed root-safe bedtime-tale hutch.

We realist rabbits wrongly denigrate
the softhearted order of your careful state.

LATE SPRING AS USUAL

The green vine is moving.
The motion's too slow to be
visible but it is racing,
racing feeling for a way
across the wall of fence
it's scrawling on, inches added every day.
Forwarding, sunwarding, it claims
its place. Green states its claim. It writes
the lesson of the day: longing,
longing coming true while arcing
out and up according to the instruction
of desire. Sun-hungry its tip has tilted
toward sun-space. Already
it is speeding leaf-notes out of its root
all along the sprigless budless thread
still scribbling the deed of its location.
In two weeks or one or four

morning   glory.

THE WOLF AND THE LAMB

La raison du plus fort est toujours la meilleure

FROM JEAN DE LA FONTAINE, *FABLES* I, 10

The strongest reasons are the reasons of the strong.
It's so—as we'll show before long.

A lamb was drinking quietly
close to the edge of a clear brook
which was on the path the wolf, when fasting, took.
The wolf eyed the lamb hungrily.
"Who's made you so brave you muddy my drink?" he cried,
cross as two sticks and fit to be tied.
"Such arrogance must be punished, don't you agree?"
"Sire," said the lamb, "may it please Your High Majesty
to be unenraged—and to note
that where I stand and wet my throat
is—as you, Sire, may see is true—
downstream from you,
downstream by twenty yards at least,
proof I can't possibly muddy your royal drink
from my low stance here at the brink."
"Wretch! You DO muddy it—and," said the cruel beast,
"what's worse, you told lots of lies about me last year."
"Not I! This year's my first; last year I wasn't here,"
said the lamb. "I'm still nursing my mother."
"Not you? Then it was your brother!"
"I have none."
                    "Then one of your kin.
You owe me, one way or the other,
you, your shepherd, your dogs, their kin—
I must take revenge. Your crimes are known."
Wolf dragged lamb under the trees
and cracked and ate him, blood and bone,
with no further formalities.

TO THE WINDS, FROM A WINNOWER OF WHEAT

Translated from Joachim du Bellay, in honor of William Ryding

Welcome, welcome, infant breeze,
lightly flying where you please.
Whisperer, why not whistle, too,
among the sun-struck grass.
Teach it to bend when you pass;
push less gently through.

I bring you these spring beauties,
lilies, violets, daisies,
and these notable roses,
these rosy briar clusters
whose split buds match the luster
this carnation discloses.

May your crescent breath soon reign
strong and clear across this plain.
Freshen this spot, where I stay
to work the wheat. I obey
the one true winnowing way
in the heat of the day.

LISTEN

clouds:
are they all
    soundless

(are you sure?)

A RUNE, INTERMINABLE

Low above the moss
a sprig of scarlet berries
soon eaten or blackened
tells time.

> Go to a wedding
> as to a funeral:
> bury the loss.

> Go to a funeral
> as to a wedding:
> marry the loss.

> Go to a coming
> as to a going:
> unhurrying.

Time is winter-green.
Seeds keep time.
Time, so kept, carries us
across to no-time where

no time is lost.

ROUTE 80, SALT LAKE CITY TO RENO, BEAUTIFUL

for Ann Cosler Gallagher

The man at the dry gas station says he can recall,
maybe every nine or ten years, a hard rain then a rush
of carpeting flowers up sudden & small.

Not lately. And the dust-maker sun, alkaline
over a wound-scouring wind, sees to it
the flowers seed but leave no green sign.

This seascape of stone, its beige & grey stretched exposed
to ten hundred thousand winters, records
no events but those of rocks: WE EXPLODED—

announcing it in a seared continuous cry

to the vastness of empty unlistening
others call sky.

WALKING HOME FROM THE MUSEUM

The pleasure of walking, Brother Angel,
calls to mind your Paradise panel
of radiant saviors. They step the vertical
at ease in their deathlife, delectable.
You show among slow green leaves their bliss in place
in the vivid repose of each breathless face.

I lack leaves and their air-exchanging grace.
I lack gold leaf and your burin skill. Here I walk
east and west of death, toward their lute-led talk,
its pure sound spilt from song. In their words' embrace
strangers partner. Their redeeming speech spans
time and tune. Solo, they also move as a throng
conversing, hand lifted to open hand,
their speech sung as if not split from song.

II

WE OWN THE ALTERNATIVE

for Naomi Replansky, poet, and OWN, the Old Women's Network

"Mere failure to be young is not interesting,"
our host says. "Here we are free to be not young,
not bound to evaluate everything,
ready for Tuesday's flimsy shift to be flung
over Friday's shoulder, or for it to cling,
a comfort when cold winds make comfort disappear.

Old's our game. We've fought clear of innocence.
So we dress our acts up, or down. We veer
from chitchat to epics of our consequence.
Old lefty post-docs can read as they appear
words of doom or grace off the graffiti fence
of chance, and laugh out loud at what some fear.
We even grab a can and squirt our mark
now & then, in the now before then the dark."

POPULAR BINOCULARS

Opposites are mind's shorthand but don't exist
What soars from sight above, begins beneath.
Watch:
      up her beanstalk smart Jackie twists,
a climbing rose between her teeth,
to claim the virile task of Giant Slaughter
leaving her mother's milkmaid life below.

Exchanging roses with the Giant's Daughter,
she borrows Giant binoculars which show
the low world's working people, us, poor as piss,
all tired, some brave. She shouts, "My quest's below!
Come, Giant's Wife & Daughter, to Metropolis!"
They steal the Giant's stolen gold before they go.
They invest in Jackie's mother. They grow.

Two eyes yield one vision. Two sexes show
promise, like a prismatic synthesis.

SOLILOQUY AT THE BENEFIT EVENT

"The name of this performance is 'The New Wife'—
it's not about us old wives. It has to do
with 'young' meaning 'younger than.' Its set is rife
with screens for folded scenes that one miscue
might expose us to. What's her name, again?
(Wife I's our age.) She looks soft (like Wife II,
who blanked us like a hallucinogen).

Don't say, 'You know my son was at school with you.'
Poor thing. Best we just not mention children.

Wife I's better off—with debts, with custody—
without him. She'd want us to applaud
this girl, her looks, her style, his taste—though he
does look awkward, playing young, playing lord.
She's bored. He's scared. She's scared. He's bored."

CONTRACTED

Here comes her helpmeet
               at a trot.
He's a dealer in defeat;
               she is not.
Woe's what he's here for,
               not so, she,
proud of her bookstore
               at the mall.
No pride could look more
               like a fall.

DRIVE LIKE A LADY BLUES

No I won't stick to the back roads
when I go out to drive.
I'm not driving right-lane byways
just to keep that car alive.

No buzzwords no byways
no back roads no beehive. No.
I say I'm driving on the highway
at this time. I'm driving my way
on your highway, eat my dust,
Lord knows it ain't *my* tranny going bust.

TRAIN TO AVIGNON

Three international European young
homing toward Holland from Kashmir
complain, "This train stops everywhere."
They're headed for Arles to watch men stick bulls;
they think that might be interesting.

The fresh white head of my opposite number
turns from them; she inverts her smile, nods to me,
says the grand Avignon children she's going to see
handsomely repay her interest in them.

The Dutch drink Cola pop-top with their chips.
I halve a white-fleshed peach & eat summer raw.
I envy madame her unvarying knife cut;
salami & bread drop in classic rounds.

Prompt with Latin hosting courtesy,
once she learns I am a foreigner
we drink a wine, pale gold, drawn
from the grapes of her Burgundy acre.
She approves my raspberries, merely bought.

The young debate among themselves in Dutch.
Panicky, they don't know where they are. She
waits, then points (noting the asterisks
on her up-to-date non-crack train schedule)
to when they'll arrive. They sigh in relief.

She helps them endorse their rucksacks
& smiles them out into her customary world.
I've given them all my oranges.

· · ·

We, extravagant, chat easily,
take our vagrant ease. We're off,
stopping & starting, off-season,
off-peak, on time, on our own.

LAST

Waste-pipe sweat, unchecked, has stained the floor
under the kitchen sink. For twenty years
it's eased my carelessness into a mean soft place,

its dirty secret dark, in a common place.
Today the pipe's fixed. Workmen rip up the floor
that's served and nagged me all these good/bad years.

They cut and set in new boards, to last for years.
House-kept no more, I waltz out of the place
clean-shod and leave no footprint on the floor,

displaced and unfloored. This year, nothing goes to waste.

SIMPLES

what do I want

well I want to
get better

LANGUAGE ACQUISITION

Burn, or speak your mind. For the oak to untruss
its passion it must explode as fire or leaves.

The delicious tongue we speak with speaks us.
A liquor of sweetness where its root cleaves
ripens fluent, as it runs for the desirous
reason, the touching sense. The infant says "I"
like earthquake and wavers as place takes voice.
Earth steadies smiling around her, in reply
to her self-finding pronoun, her focal choice.
We wait: while sun sucks earth juices up from wry
root-runs tangled under dark, while the girl
no longer vegetal, steps into view:
a moving speaker, an "I" the air whirls
toward the green exuberance of "You."

SEPTEMBER IN NEW YORK,
PUBLIC & ELEMENTARY, 1927

As if speech could have sparks
leaping in it (the way they leap up
    when a new lover says, "Welcome home, love,"
    or a new softball captain says, "Let's go, gang!")

once upon a time she with her soft fast glance
collecting them said, "Good morning, class,"

and all her seated uplooking expectant
second-graders quickly said gladly,
"Good morning, Miss McKnight,"

ready, hearts hammering,
her gang, her lovers, her class.

ON EASTER SATURDAY BELLS WHACKED THE AIR

Pet dogs help children. Spring after spring
two blaze-white Samoyeds sped me out
to my relief to run
into a new hush after the last noon clang
of church bells, rung ringing since dawn
to proclaim Easter Saturday—
          big bells, high up, and all of them
at once, let loose, a deafening glory

for my city of muted immigrants, plenty
of Catholics, bells just a few blocks apart,
Italy, Poland, Ireland, Germany, & Spain,
their metal tested, their cast full-voiced
non-liturgic, jubilee, wake up, hear this, look
out, resurrection, halleluia in yanked abandon
all morning—
          avenue traffic drowned out,
backyards & alleys humming in soundsurge,
and my breath a strong pulse
of everywhere hooray—no synchrony
no harmony no purity just hooray

just giant jubilee noise, dogs of course
not liking it, but for me utter
exultation rampant, though I loved my dogs
and took the run they gave me exulting
This is the day that the world hath made.
Rejoice and be glad therein.

WHAT SPEAKS OUT

Massive, a musical instrument
unplayed for four thousand years,
it's almost my height, caged
in museum glass,
ticketed:
It's a kind of lute, harplike, huge,
a lute made of solid silver (blackening).
At its foot is a slack tangle of strings,
and if strung taut if touched
it would thrum.

From its baseboard stares
the head of a boar made
by someone who had seen a boar.

Cornered, caved, tarnishing
regardless in the dark at the back
edge of a royal burial, it sucked
the dust of the three skulls
of three young women
whose heads it crushed
as it was planted there.
The human remains are listed as
still in Mesopotamia, informative
though not museum-quality, dated by scraps
of ribbon, bone, dress, beads, a plectrum.
Linens and skeletons
show they were tall girls, probably
two singers and a lutanist, untarnished,
breakable, intentional, faithful
servants and instruments of song.

ORPHANED OLD

I feel less lucky since my parents died.
Father first, then mother, have left me
out in a downpour
roofless in cold wind
no umbrella no hood no hat no warm
native place, nothing
between me and eyeless sky.

In the gritty prevailing wind
I think of times I've carelessly lost things:
      that white-gold ring when I was eight,
      a classmate named Mercedes Williams,
      my passport in Gibraltar,
      my maiden name.

WHY VOW

Hopkins (some say, daft) holds
that his self is unlost, a fact,
unchanged by its unfolding
as it stands for his each act.

Self (daft or not) lives out its vow:
his now is a perpetual now.

Obedient: he said he would.
He did as he said. He did
as he was told. He could
good as gold, hold good.

MAGNANIMOUS, MAGNIFICENT

Dump the jump-cuts, gentlemen. Steady on.
Try a kick-start to warm your kept cool and
your chic smiles lightly perverti. For once,
laugh at each other's jokes, don't top them,
simmer down, take the next step.
Propose lunch, or even dinner with your wives
(waiting all this competitive time for
you to look lovable again, to come with them to table).
Take notice, praise their shaky grace. Say Please.
Lay your cards on the linen faceup
causing a music to start. Listen—
it's music for dancing, so you dance.
Say you like it. Admit you've had some good luck.
Thank your friends for arriving on time. To the others,
the ones you dream of as enemies,
smile and say Thank you, and then try to mean it.
As the music stops you'll miss its lilt.
Keep dancing, keep listening. Speak up.
Ask for more music, more. In case you don't know,
what you want is magnificent, yours for the asking,
the rhythm of magnanimous exchange.

TV, EVENING NEWS
—seen on CNN, autumn 2005, *Afghanistan*

It's a screenful of chaos but
the cameraman's getting good framing shots
from behind one woman's back.
The audio's poor. The shouts are slices of noise.
I don't know the languages.

No hot hit heroes are there.
No wicked people are there.

Achilles is not there, or Joshua either.
Rachel is not there, nor Sojourner Truth.
Iwo Jima flag boys? not there.
Twin Towers first defenders? not there.
My children are thank God not there
any more or less than you and I are not there.

I safe screen-watch. A youth
young in his uniform
signals his guard squad
twice: OK go, to the tanks
and the cameramen: OK go.

The tank takes the house wall.
The house genuflects. The tank proceeds.
The house kneels. The roof dives.
The woman howls. Dust rises.
They cut to the next shot.

The young men and the woman
breathe the dust of the house

which now is its prayer.
A dust cloud rises, at one
with the prayer of all the kneeling houses
asking to be answered
and answerable anywhere.

III

THANK GERARD

Cascade: rain torrential rain
waterfalls down our stone façade.

Our fields lately fire-parched
now glossy cross the flat rise
you ploughed earlier. The whole
length of one sillion-streak gleams

Gerard

cut-stroke the sillion the gash
we have in mind is your mind
                    lifting muck-life
turned sunstruck to each side
silvershot at low sunset after the rain
every drop cataract
is not this the rain
we have longed for, you and I

                    God   to you
                    hold him close-folded
                    above his sillion
                    Loft him Halo him
                    Prize him high, pen in hand
                    his two uprooted feet
                    flailing awkward rain-streaked

                    below his healing blooded knees.

THE GOOD

The plot is simple: a traveling man
is mugged on a lonely street, robbed, beaten,
and left to bleed. The few who hear his groans
won't stop. They don't want to get sucked in.
Then he hears someone: a Samaritan
salesman from the ghetto. He groans again
& it works. He's saved.
                  As I gnaw this old bone
I sink to the marrow: my late father, in sudden
fresh recall. He said righteousness is shown
less by the short halt to help a stranger than
by evoking others' genius, then going on
to do the work that he knew was his own.

Mercy praises Justice: the Samaritan
acts to do exactly all he can.

AGAINST FIERCE SECRETS

Only to themselves are the passionate
hot. To the objects of their passion they
are cold. What Yeats knew. They eradicate
what they notice, as the thumb hard-crams the clay
impressionable under it, to lie flat,
apt to the shape their cold-steel scribes may
cut or spurn it to. Yet they know passion
must drown to ripen sweet & give fair play
to the whole life hot passion speeds us from.

As passion's object, dig with your ampersand:
be cold & hot. The receptive earth will come
to transform the root-end that your planting hand
cut & abandoned, to new chrysanthemum.

Heartfelt thought, drop your guard, keep clear, be slow;
double your careful opposites & grow.

ON LINE

Over the rootspread of woods, words, turf
we walk, talking, through the blue hour.
In each of us, the rootspreads outline
a universe at its origin.

We reach the lakeshore.
We row out into the dark.
We fish all night, no nets. Sometimes
we weight or bait each other's hooks,
testing what our lines can catch.

May the lakelife prosper.
May the hooks we remove
    do minimal damage.
May the lines hold good.

COMETING

I like to drink my language in
straight up, no ice no twist no spin
—no fruity phrases, just unspun
words trued right toward a nice
idea, for chaser. True's a risk.
Take it I say. Do true for fun.

We say water is taught by thirst
       earth by ocean diving
       birds by the lift of the heart

       oh that lift
       —curative, isn't it—
       a surge a sursum   as
       words become us
       we come alive lightly
       saying Oh

at the wordstream of sentences
transparent in their consequence
cometing before our eyes
trailing crystalline
across our other sky
and we drink from it
       for the jolt of language
       for its lucid hit
       of bliss, the surprise.

FRANCE, AS FIRST DAUGHTER OF ROME

The tiny hillchurch that would, if full, hold
some thirty folk, is locked and disaffected
from the cult, save for one day a year when
on the feast of its saint a priest drives in
to suit up & celebrate the Mass,
bloodless after two thousand bloody years.
Grumbling, pairs of villagers shift gears
to reach church in first gear, though that wastes gas.
At home, on low heat, dinner simmers;
they've put their old-time pre-TV faces on,
left pills & condoms shelved by the bedstead.

They de-car here where the rite will unfold
its gestures meant to localize infinity

as one old man knows.
                    One may be plenty.

ART: OLD AS NEW

When wishes composed me
but couldn't come true,
when dreams spoke girl-Latin
(well, I was new)

I met works of genius
expectant and thirsty.
I still do. So do you.
Still unimproved, thirsty, expectant,
we house them remembered
inside, where armed and endangered,
we live by the replay that gratifies
the thirst it rectifies.

WHAT *IS* IS

True high is true deep.
True pebble's true stone.
She is not a true sheep.
She is a true clone.

RECOVERY

I recover my history
and my chairs
with brilliant fabrics,
putting on airs
of luminous usefulness
and captivating pattern.
Of course, my dears,
they can't be sat in.

FOR ROBERT RAUSCHENBERG

The door I bought is a door with three lights.
A door with three lights is nonetheless
solid, somewhat, penetrated and yet
sometimes somewhat impassable.
Open or shut it's part opaque,
part holey, like me not definite,
so I'll hang this door gladly.
I admit the doors of perception are
cleansed only momently as
they open in on the ward of light.

      invitational: do come, light.
               shadow, do come, do.

      institutional: here's the clean-up squad;
               here's the vinegary window-washer;
               here's the hopeful tidier-upper;
    please indicate where they should begin.

Shouldering aside the praising critic,
the painter explains, "Much to see
but not much showing."

BLISS AND GRIEF

No one
is here
right now.

SKEPTIC

for Helen DeMott, painter of waves

"I watch the heaving moving
of great waters. I read their surfaces.
Motion patterns them. Water
expresses the sea floor it is moved by.

Language thinks us. Myth or mouth
we migrants are its mystery.
It's our tension floats those halcyons
we want to say are safe
riding the wave-swell,
on the surface of some sea."

"Try telling that to the lookout sailor
his ship headed into the storm
headed for floundering.
Oh, I believe in storms all right,

and in ships that skim or sink,
and in some birds, some sailors.

But a scupper of a place of peace,
a nest-sized cupping and two
lovebirds calm in it?
No matter how much we want such peace,
no matter who believes in it (mouth or myth)
the tale of peace in a love nest in stormcalm
would only bewilder

us crow's nest sailors looking ahead
about to drown."

TRANSPORT

The rose, for all its behavior,
is smaller than the lifelove it stands for,
only briefly brightening,
and even its odor
only a metaphor.
Or so we suppose
just as we suppose the savior
we employ or see next door
is only some hired man
gardening.

IMAGINING STARRY

The place of language is the place between me
and the world of presences I have lost
—complex country, not flat. Its elements free-
float, coherent for luck to come across;
its lines curve as in a mental orrery
implicit with stars in active orbit,
only their slowness or swiftness lost to sense.
The will dissolves here. It becomes the infinite
air of imagination that stirs immense
among losses and leaves me less desolate.
Breathing it I spot a sentence or a name,
a rescuer, charted for recovery,
to speak against the daily sinking flame
& the shrinking waters of the mortal sea.

MIGRANT AMONG US

The otherworld is this world heeded
so well it swims in close to us,
its echo and shadow a swivel
of unintended attention.

Take notice: the otherworld
is lustrous, like sealight or
twilight, ambiguous because
it's more than one thing at a time:

> like the summer forward-thrust
> of the rackety local rivulet
> hurrying its loud brown
> water to its little fall,

> or like those of us who both

> track the stars and also
> fly earthward at night
> like migrant bird flocks—

as if the dark were flared,
as if we can see in the dark,
and we almost can.

REACHING

My plane takes off on time, and so do I.
The journey it charts charts me as I fly;
sight flashes into thought. I stare in at it
though (mapped as thought-through) the map lines lie
loopy. Thought goes too far, stretching to explain
my self, its selves, and how they move to unify.
They rush to catch the bright becoming point
thought casts before them like a light to work by.

The plane's nose always gets there first. I sit
belated, in the cabin section of the plane.
I'm my observer. I maneuver to join
my old self to its avant-garde, my eyes.
Sight likes travel which likes fresh surprises.
Self likes surprise that undoes old disguises.

TESTING GARDENING

In the garden I watch myself take care
as if I were the garden. I even learn
from experience! Slowly (fair is fair),
I may grow less stupid and learn to turn
error to advantage—though mistakes take
years of uprooting seedlings sprung from seed
dropped a decade ago in error's long wake.
I was right to want you, to sweat, weed,
balance acid soil, shield you from sunscald
early, then prune to make sure the sun you need
found you. For these few spring weeks you're a sprawl
of flowers, you green the summer toward its rest
in fruited autumn. Yet it's winter that's best,

yes, to imagine joy, next. The winter test.

PHYSICAL TRAINING

Spelled out in the body, history is slow.
My label reads: cryptic amateur, adept
at dailiness. Crow's-feet, muscles, scars have kept
the record of its waves, high tide and low.
I begin to learn to read its common sense:
> Sun-squint breakfast foreplay. Triumphs. Defeats.
> Lobster bisque. The wet-wash weight of linen sheets.
> Freeborn words. The broken kitchen. The open air
> of public walkways . . .
> > > I read the honey-striped
turn of body caught off guard, its full text ripe.
Its random list or life is in good repair.
Grateful, grateful, my hand slow to turn the page
turns it, labeled grateful, already engaged.

DANCING DAY I

At the horizon's lit fog rim
earth keeps in touch with sky.
I call this the end of the beginning.

In its mist, frayed ghosts of selves drowse;
I call them my lost selves.
Lately they drift close, unaging,
watching me age. Now & then, one or some

flare up, known shapes in known clothes.
Each of them is not not me, and wears
the clothes I walked in, joked, worked hurt in,

as I played my sweet pipsqueak part
paradiddle on the hi-hat.
I still know all those moves.

I begin to remember; I remember them,
some from when my father was alive.
A deep breath taken. Restorative.
They hum soft part-songs, hard to hear.

And now they're singing. They've come to stay!
It's turning into a party.

I put out bread, plates, glasses, grapes,
apples, napkins, pretzels, Bleu des Causses.

They whistle old signals. In our one name
we agree to our selving. I do agree.
                        I'll propose a toast,
why not. Time to let go. Get going.
Out of the cellar I take, ripe,
the rest of the case of Clos de Vougeot.

DANCING DAY II

Once, one made many.
Now, many make one.
The rest is requiem.

We're running out of time, so
we're hurrying home to
practice to
gether for the general dance.
We're past get-ready, almost at get-set.
Here we come many to
dance as one.

Plenty more lost selves keep arriving, some
we weren't waiting for. We stretch and
lace up practice shoes. We mind our manners—
no staring, just snatching a look
            —strict and summative—
at each other's feet & gait & port.

Every one we ever were shows up
with world-flung poor triumphs
flat in the backpacks we set down to greet
each other. Glad tired gaudy
we are more than we thought
& as ready as we'll ever be.

We've all learned the moves, separately,

from the absolute dancer
      the foregone deep breather
the original choreographer.

                        .   .   .

Imitation's limitation—but who cares.
We'll be at our best on dancing day.
                    On dancing day
we'll belt out tunes we'll step to
together
till it's time for us to say
there's nothing more to say
        nothing to pay   no way
        pay no mind   pay no heed
        pay as we go.
Many is one; we're out of here,
exeunt omnes,
        exit   oh and save
        this last dance for me

on the darkening ground
looking up into
the last hour of left light
in the star-stuck east,
its vanishing flective, bent
breathlessly.

NEW POEMS (2016)

CELEBRATION

Light began in September to streak the slant.
Now it unseals in the Spring, wilfully singing the realm of separate
    design.
It picks up the speed of streaming recall
and takes us off post-equinox able to signify.

Or so I guess: Ninety is old, I
keep telling myself, so behave! And I'm older, 94. It is the look of
    happy
95, blue, grey, though cold. It gives
a green expectation and I taste.

NOT TO BE SEEN

Where's air? It's placeless. Birds take place in it;
birdsong commutes there between star shine and ground
along net-waved bird paths, out of our sight.

Air that I'm out in shows me sight.
I breathe, in its temperate embrace. It
fires my blood, I wingless on the ground.

Air envelops earth, easy above ground,
donor of bird-color, medium of sight.
All my life I prize it, thirsty for it,

sight-giver, ground-keeper. We drink it in.

AUNT GRACE WEARS BEAUTIFUL CLOTHES

Asleep, she has no idea she is old.

She's running uphill, no lightfoot, but quite fast
past the houses and driveways of family friends
toward the higher fields just breaking into flower
that weren't there before, when she was awake.
She stops at the tree edge. The sight that yields
is daisies. Careful she enters the pathless field
of daisies daisies hundreds sunning. She takes
her time. She crouches among their stems. Bowered
low, she looks up at their heads, their far sky.
The wind's soft. The sunclock's high. It can't last.
Aunt Grace is coming to lunch, she's been told.
Good. Maybe bring her a love-me-not daisy or
love-me. Aunt Grace will know what daisies are for.

NEXT

Just as we know we're all Isaac
we are all of us Abraham
no kidding

Kierkegaard's leap of faith
                        domesticated.

Drop the jump-rope
get naked
                   jump
off the cliff

(down time
not much)

ART OF THE CAVE

A carbon-dater scientist
was peering close and
(lucky, lucky!) he saw, left behind or lost,
a whistle.
He found on stony ground
a hollow bone, pierced
as a mouthpiece, thirty-five
thousand years, not
ghost but aliveable
a token for fingertips.

Someone made a replica.
Someone whistled it, a cosmic ride, ours.

Here we are, human. A sound found sounding.
Lucky. Human is here.

AIR AS ADJUSTMENT

dedicated to John Rawls

I

Mighty Planet Earth
orbits in order, its greened blues
attractive in our aerial envelope:
Lawful, obedient,
it turns among
stars and astral junk.
Earth bears with us undismissing.
Enveloped, we hear it thrum.
                    We're all over it.

We think of Earth as ours. We
were raised here. Its bloodstream
slung in our knotty salty nets,
seconds the continuous bass
of the pulse of the spheres.

2

On foot I am in
the fight of my life
facing my enemy.

I duck and fall side-
ways to the commons,
a space a narrow strip an edge:
Tiny, it's enough.

Quieter, I inch away from the struggle.

Behind my enemy and
behind me, our landscape,
erupted, lies wide, hurt.
Now what.

Here I stand (life, here saved).
He too doesn't fall. (it's disarming.)

Behind my, enemy, his country
like mine behind me,
broken smokes in the sun.

We've reached the verge. We
overlap We catch our breath and
stop bristling.   We speak.

I can see him better from here.
We overlap. We word our overlap
forward from our verge.

Air holds us, fond.

both of us speaking and
audible on our equal overlap,

both of us Earthling
under the hugely overlapping sun.

Index of Titles

Index of First Lines

A NOTE ABOUT THE AUTHOR

Marie Ponsot, the winner of *Poetry* magazine's Ruth Lilly Prize for lifetime achievement and the Frost Medal from the Poetry Society of America, was born in 1921. She is the author of six previous collections, including *The Bird Catcher,* winner of the National Book Critics Circle Award for poetry. A professor emerita of English at Queens College, CUNY, she also taught at the Unterberg Poetry Center of the 92nd Street Y, the New School University, and Beijing Univerity. Ponsot is a chancellor of the Academy of American Poets and lives in New York City.

A NOTE ON THE TYPE

Pierre Simon Fournier *le jeune* (1712–1768), who designed the type used in this book, was both an originator and a collector of types. His services to the art of printing were his design of letters, his creation of ornaments and initials, and his standardization of type sizes. In 1764 and 1766 he published his *Manuel typographique*, a treatise on the history of French types and printing, on typefounding in all its details, and on what many consider his most important contribution to typography—the measurement of type by the point system.

Typeset by North Market Street Graphics, Lancaster, Pennsylvania

Printed and bound by Berryville Graphics, Berryville, Virginia

Designed by Betty Lew